Praise for *Beyond Pizzas & Pies* . . .

The authors are right on—developing "fraction sense" is one of the most difficult tasks of new (or experienced) teachers. This book and the accompanying video clips provide a wonderful resource for helping teachers help their students become truly fluent with fractions.

> —*Barbara Reys, President*
> *Curators' Professor and Lois Knowles Faculty Fellow*
> *University of Missouri, Columbia, Missouri*

Beyond Pizzas & Pies is smart, accessible, and usable. McNamara and Shaughnessy assemble the key resources and insights teachers need to help students develop robust understanding of fractions. Clear explanations of the specific mathematical ideas and research on key challenges for learners are coordinated with focused instructional tasks and detailed guidance for their use in the classroom. The tasks develop complex mathematical proficiency by combining work on concepts with skill development and the ability to use representations and to reason about fractions.

> —*Deborah Loewenberg Ball, William H. Payne Collegiate Professor,*
> *School of Education, University of Michigan*

McNamara and Shaughnessy's splendid work guides student understanding of fractions by engaging them in a relevant and thoughtful method. The authors bridge fundamental gaps between concept and application, using challenging and fun exercises that demonstrate these principals through visual and hands-on activities. *Beyond Pizzas & Pies* is an outstanding guide to a difficult unit on which so many mathematical concepts rely.

> —*Rebecca Gris, GATE teacher, grades 2–3*
> *Boise Schools, Boise, Idaho*

This book addresses not just what students *should* learn about fractions, but how children actually think, where that thinking comes from, and what teachers can do to make their instruction more effective. Each chapter is carefully structured to present the research base as well as classroom activities that can immediately be put to use. I can't wait to use the book and video clips with my preservice teachers, since they summarize the most essential (and usable) information about the teaching and learning of fractions.

> —*Laurie Edwards, Professor of Education*
> *Saint Mary's College of California*

Julie and Meghan have provided a multimedia resource rich in both mathematics content and pedagogical content. They clearly identify common student misconceptions about fractions and, even more importantly, offer practical ideas and activities to help deepen students' essential understanding of fractions!

> —*Josh Rosen, Math Specialist*
> *Dobbs Ferry School District, New York*

This book and video clips lay out explicit strategies and activities for developing fraction understanding. The research, mathematics, and pedagogy are vividly brought to life through classroom scenarios and examples that will resonate with teachers.

> —*Carne Barnett-Clarke, Director*
> *Math Pathways & Pitfalls, WestEd*

Julie and Meghan's multimedia resource forces educators to acknowledge that the traditional way of teaching fractions is limiting, lacking opportunity for higher-level application. They offer concrete solutions that can be easily integrated into any classroom curriculum.

—Lindsay Phillips, eighth-grade teacher
Portsmouth Middle School, Portsmouth, Rhode Island

Beyond Pizzas & Pies expertly presents the essential concepts that third-, fourth-, and fifth-grade teachers must fully understand so they can teach students to develop a deep conceptual understanding of fractions. By presenting ten critical strategies for developing fraction sense, McNamara and Shaughnessy provide a tightly scaffolded plan for both teachers and students that is easy to follow and goes well beyond the usual teacher manuals and math texts commonly used in upper elementary school classrooms.

—Maggie Riddle, Director of Schools,
Berkeley Unified School District, California

McNamara and Shaughnessy understand the difficulty of fractions in mathematics education and masterfully weave together classroom vignettes, the latest in education research, mathematics, and classroom lessons in easy-to-follow chapters that will challenge your assumptions about how to teach this critically important topic. This multimedia resource is a goldmine of information delivered in simple, straightforward language.

—Jennifer M. Langer-Osuna, PhD, Assistant Professor
Stanford University, Stanford, California

Using these activities has increased my students' deep understanding of fractions and their math confidence, while decreasing their confusion when we discuss decimals. I needed this resource when I started teaching thirty years ago!

—Morri Spang, fifth-grade teacher,
San Pedro St. Elementary School, Los Angeles, California

McNamara and Shaughnessy have created a gem of a resource for teaching the very difficult content area of fractions. This book and the accompanying video clips are guaranteed to support teachers in developing deeper understandings of the complexities involved in reasoning about and computing with fractions, so that they in turn can support the developing understandings of their students.

—Mary Q. Foote, Assistant Professor of Mathematics Education
Queens College, CUNY, New York

Bravo to the clever authors of *Beyond Pizzas & Pies* for serving both *teachers and students* a practical menu with fresh recipes of applicable strategies that will help *us* think outside the pie. The explanations backed by research stimulated and altered my own math sense, empowering my instruction with more purpose and comprehension. My fifth graders will be challenged and charmed as *we all* deepen our fraction knowledge.

—Karen L. Thompson, fifth-grade teacher
Farrand Elementary, Plymouth, Michigan

Beyond Pizzas & Pies

SECOND EDITION

10 Essential Strategies for Supporting Fraction Sense

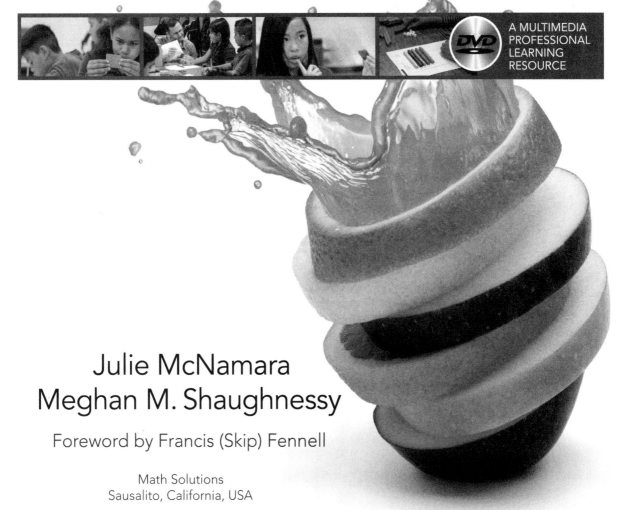

A MULTIMEDIA
PROFESSIONAL
LEARNING
RESOURCE

DVD

Julie McNamara
Meghan M. Shaughnessy

Foreword by Francis (Skip) Fennell

Math Solutions
Sausalito, California, USA

Math Solutions
One Harbor Drive, Suite 101
Sausalito, California, USA 94965
www.mathsolutions.com

The publisher gratefully acknowledges adapted material:

Chapter 5: Activity 5.2 "What's the Unit?" was adapted from *Teaching Fractions and Ratios for Understanding: Essential Content Knowledge and Instructional Strategies for Teachers, 2d ed.*, by Susan J. Lamon. Copyright 2005 by Susan J. Lamon. Adapted with permission from Taylor and Francis Group, LLC, a division of Informa plc.

Chapter 6: Activity 6.3 "Fractions and Decimals Flip" was adapted from "The Empty Number Line: A Useful Tool or Just Another Procedure?" by Janette Bobis, *Teaching Children Mathematics* 13(8): 410–23, with permission from *Teaching Children Mathematics*, copyright 2007, by the National Council of Teachers of Mathematics. All rights reserved.

Chapter 8: Excerpt from "Establishing Fraction Benchmarks" by Barbara J. Reys, Ok-Kyeong Kim, and Jennifer M. Bay, *Mathematics Teaching in the Middle School* 4(8): 530–32 is reprinted with permission from *Mathematics Teaching in the Middle School*, copyright 1999, by the National Council of Teachers of Mathematics. All rights reserved.

Library of Congress Cataloging-in-Publication Data

McNamara, Julie.
  Beyond pizzas & pies : 10 essential strategies for supporting fraction sense, grades 3–5 / Julie McNamara and Meghan M. Shaughnessy ; foreword by Francis (Skip) Fennell. — Second edition.
    pages cm
  Includes bibliographical references and index.
  ISBN 978-1-935099-53-6 (pbk.) — ISBN 1-935099-53-1 (pbk.)
1. Fractions—Study and teaching (Elementary) 2.   Ratio and proportion—Study and teaching (Elementary) I. Shaughnessy, Meghan M. II. Title. III. Title: Beyond pizzas and pies. IV. Title: Fraction sense, grades 3–5.
  QA117.M265 2015
  372.7'2—dc23   2014046879

Editor: Jamie Ann Cross
Production: Denise A. Botelho
Cover design: Jan Streitburger, Crescent Hill Studio
Interior design: Lisa Delgado, Delgado and Company
Composition: Publishers' Design and Production Services, Inc.
Cover images: © ifong/Shutterstock.com
Interior images: Friday's Films

1 2 3 4 5 6 7 8 9 10   31   24 23 22 21 20 19 18 17 16 15

A Message from Math Solutions

We at Math Solutions believe that teaching math well calls for increasing our understanding of the math we teach, seeking deeper insights into how students learn mathematics, and refining our lessons to best promote students' learning.

Math Solutions shares classroom-tested lessons and teaching expertise from our faculty of professional development consultants as well as from other respected math educators. Our publications are part of the nationwide effort we've made since 1984 that now includes

- more than five hundred face-to-face professional development programs each year for teachers and administrators in districts across the country;
- professional development books that span all math topics taught in kindergarten through high school;
- videos for teachers and for parents that show math lessons taught in actual classrooms;
- on-site visits to schools to help refine teaching strategies and assess student learning; and
- free online support, including grade-level lessons, book reviews, inservice information, and district feedback, all in our Math Solutions Online Newsletter.

For information about all of the products and services we have available, please visit our website at *www.mathsolutions.com.* You can also contact us to discuss math professional development needs by calling (800) 868-9092 or by sending an email to *info@mathsolutions.com.*

We're always eager for your feedback and interested in learning about your particular needs. We look forward to hearing from you.

Contents

Activities

Activity-Specific Reproducibles

Reproducibles Used with More Than One Activity

I f there is a foundational building block for understanding fractions, considering fractions as numbers gets my vote. The Common Core State Standards for Mathematics' focus on fractions as number within the Number and Operations—Fractions content domain underscores this importance. And, yes as learners experience, understand, and develop proficiency with fractions a sense of number emerges: Fraction Sense, the desired prerequisite for developing understanding and proficiency, even fluency, with operations involving fractions and decimals, and the readiness for middle grade work with ratio and proportion.

The second edition of *Beyond Pizzas & Pies*, like the first edition, addresses a major challenge for every third- through fifth-grade teacher I have ever met. Fractions—defined as *a/b* fractions, decimals, and related percents—are important building blocks for higher-level mathematics. This edition also includes video clips of students filmed in actual classrooms who are engaged in a sampling of the book's activities, thus providing more professional development opportunities for this amazing resource. I could go on and on here, but allow me to provide just a few indicators as to the importance of fractions as numbers—considering partitioning/sharing, equivalence, use of varied representations, and comparing and ordering fractions as elements of these prerequisites of fraction sense and necessary prior to extensive work with operations involving "these" numbers (a/b fractions and decimals).

- In 2008, more than 740 teachers of algebra responded to a National Mathematics Advisory Panel survey about the preparation of their students for algebra. Teachers identified rational numbers as a major area of concern, and the Panel listed proficiency with fractions as a major goal for preK–8 mathematics education.
- Only 50 percent of eighth-grade students successfully arranged $\frac{2}{7}$, $\frac{1}{12}$, and $\frac{5}{9}$ from least to greatest (NAEP 2004).
- Only 29 percent of seventeen-year-old students translated 0.029 as 29/1000 (NAEP 2004).
- Finally, while we all have our favorite fraction stories, consider this one. I once asked a fifth grader where I might place $\frac{9}{5}$ on a number line, the student insisted that this could not be done, "because nine-fifths is more than one." By implication, number lines end at 1!

As we consider the "curricular fit" of a/b fractions, decimals, percent, and their middle grade extensions involving ratio, rate, and proportion, we must attend to the need for teachers to address foundational fraction concepts. Check that off—this book does continues to do this—and the access to classroom videos makes it even better! Take a look at each chapter. First, note how fractions are approached with early opportunities involving partitioning and sharing (which, by the way, is far too frequently disregarded in typical curricular expectations). Next, see the progression toward the importance of equivalence, comparing, and ordering, and making sense of fractions and their more frequently used equivalent: decimals. In addition, this amazing resource examines contexts where, yep, sometimes you'd rather have $\frac{1}{3}$ than $\frac{2}{3}$. And it also considers the appropriateness of particular representations, a particularly important topic for those implementing the Common Core State Standards for Mathematics (CCSSM).

Importantly, Julie McNamara and Meghan Shaughnessy have found a way not only to insert important research into this work but also to blend it with the issues addressed. And this is done on a consistent basis. I am a firm believer that we must all attend to research, and this book exemplifies the phrase linking research to practice. Even the title grabs me: you'd better believe that foundational work with fractions is beyond the overused references of pizzas and varied and sundry other pies!

At this writing, schools are in the implementation stage of the Common Core State Standards for Mathematics. However, whether you are following the Common Core, your own state's standards or your district's adopted textbook, this resource has got you covered. All fractions are important, and *Beyond Pizzas & Pies* examines the foundations necessary for all students.

I am going to continue to use this book—a lot (I keep one copy at home and one at the office for easy access)! It will be at my side as I think about fractions as critically important mathematical knowledge for teaching. *Beyond Pizzas & Pies* and the accompanying DVD will also help me think of ideas for professional development, for teaching, and for continuing the quest we all have for our students: developing number sense and ensuring that number sense extends to fractions—Fraction Sense. Thanks, Julie and Meghan.

—Francis (Skip) Fennell, L. Stanley Bowlsbey Professor
of Education & Graduate and Professional Studies,
McDaniel College Westminster, Maryland, and Past President,
National Council of Teachers of Mathematics Project
Director: Elementary Mathematics Specialists and
Teachers Leaders Project, MathSpecialists.org

VIDEO CLIP

Introduction

Watch the video clip "Introduction." Talk with a friend or colleague; what do you see in the introduction that makes you most excited about *Beyond Pizzas & Pies, Second Edition*?

Why This Resource?

If you ask an upper elementary teacher to name the most challenging mathematics topic for students, chances are you'll hear, "Fractions." Many middle school teachers find they have to review fraction concepts and operations before their students can successfully tackle algebra. We've spoken to countless adults who will unabashedly claim they hate fractions and always have. Sadly, students without a strong understanding of fractions find it difficult to progress very far in mathematics. In fact, the California State University/University of California Mathematics Diagnostic Testing Project Workgroup has found that there is a strong positive correlation between students' understanding of fractions and their overall success in mathematics (Gomez 2009). According to the Final Report of the National Mathematics Advisory Panel (2008), understanding fractions is a "foundation skill essential to success with algebra" (3). The report also states that completion of Algebra II correlates highly with future academic success as well as earning potential.

This book and the accompanying video clips are intended to support you as you help your students develop their fraction sense. Fraction sense implies a deep and flexible understanding of fractions that is not dependent on any one context or type of problem. Fraction sense is tied to common sense: Students with fraction sense can reason about fractions and don't apply rules and procedures blindly; nor do they give nonsensical answers to problems involving fractions. Because we believe that fraction sense is an essential component for students' success with fraction operations, this book and the accompanying video clips focus primarily on helping students build foundational fraction concepts.

Why Is Understanding Fractions So Hard?

In order to support your goal to help students develop what we call "Fraction Sense," we first need to identify some of the reasons that so many children and adults have such difficulty with fractions.

Helping students develop a deep and flexible understanding of fractions is a complex endeavor. In order for students to understand fractions and fraction notation, they must be able to think about numbers in a different way than when they are working with whole numbers. For example, instead of viewing a number such as 34 as representing a specific quantity, when the same digits (3 and 4) are used in the number $\frac{3}{4}$, the digits 3 and 4 represent a relationship. In addition, students need to consider the context in which the number $\frac{3}{4}$ occurs. While the relationship between the numerator 3 and the denominator 4 doesn't change across contexts, the way the fraction is represented does.

When considering $\frac{3}{4}$ as a number, the 3 represents three one-fourths, and the whole, or unit, is one.

Research identifies several factors that likely contribute to students' difficulties with fractions, including but not limited to:

- The way that fractions are written (Ball 1993; Davydov and Tsvetkovich 1991; Lamon 2007; National Research Council 2001; Smith 2002);

- Classroom practices designed to help students make sense of fraction values and notation that inadvertently mask the meaning of fractions (Armstrong and Larson 1995; Davydov and Tsvetkovich 1991; Lamon 2007; Mack 1990, 1995);

- Students' overreliance on whole number knowledge (Mack 1990; Saxe et al. 2007); and

- The many meanings of fractions, such as measure and ratio (Lamon 2001; National Research Council 2001).

When considering $\frac{3}{4}$ as part of an area, the 3 represents three replications of the area that is one-fourth of the whole.

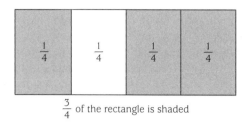

$\frac{3}{4}$ of the rectangle is shaded

When $\frac{3}{4}$ is considered as a measure, the 3 is three iterations of the distance that is one-fourth of the whole.

When $\frac{3}{4}$ is considered as part of a set, the 3 could mean three items, six items, twenty-four items, and so on, depending on the size of the entire set.

How This Resource Is Organized

This book is not necessarily intended to be read from cover to cover. Each chapter discusses one common dilemma that students have with fractions and includes classroom strategies and activities for preventing and addressing these dilemmas. Different chapters may have different levels of significance for you, depending on your grade level and your students' particular needs. The order in which you read the chapters doesn't matter; each chapter is written to stand alone.

Each of the eight chapters follows the same format:

- *CCSS Connections:* Chapters open with connections to the relevant Common Core State Standards.
- *Classroom Scenario:* Each chapter identifies a dilemma that students encounter as they begin their formal study of fractions. Some of these

dilemmas may be tied to fraction notation, some may be connected to students' previous experiences with fractions, and some may be the result of misapplying rules and procedures students learned when working with whole numbers. Each dilemma is presented in the context of a fictional classroom episode in the third-grade classroom of Mr. Burnett, the fourth-grade classroom of Ms. Alvarez, or the fifth-grade classroom of Ms. Chu. While the exact episodes and students are fictional, the students' comments and struggles are taken from our work in classrooms as either teacher or researcher. The dilemmas are also not grade-level specific; you may find that your fifth graders struggle in the same way as Mr. Burnett's third graders or your third graders may have the same difficulties as Ms. Alvarez's fourth graders.

● *What's the Math?* This section is intended to clarify the mathematics that is being addressed in each chapter.

● *What's the Research?* As teachers are asked to do more and more during the school day, it's imperative that we no longer continue with practices because "that's the way we've always done things." The research helps us to identify those strategies, contexts, and representations that may be problematic and/or limited, as well as those that will ensure we get the most out of our instructional time.

● *Classroom Activities:* Each chapter includes activities designed to help your students develop their fraction sense. Materials lists, reproducibles, and examples of student projects are included. *In addition, the accompanying video clips feature actual classroom footage of students and teachers engaged in several of the Classroom Activities.* These activities are not meant to replace your current curriculum, but you may find that they will allow you to provide experiences for your students that help them further develop their fraction sense.

● *Wrapping It Up:* Each chapter ends with closing comments, study questions, and suggestions for additional resources when appropriate.

● *Video Clips:* Chapters 2, 3, 5, and 8 include video clips that were filmed in actual classrooms; see the tables on pages xxxi–xxxiv for a listing of clips by grade and chapter.

What's New to the Second Edition?

The second edition of *Beyond Pizzas & Pies* is updated to reflect the authors' most current thinking and research. In addition, the second edition now includes 30 video clips filmed in actual classrooms. Clips range from 1 minute to 6 minutes in length with a total viewing time of approximately 70 minutes.

The 10 Essential Strategies

Following is an overview of the eight main ideas discussed in each of the chapters plus two additional strategies that permeate throughout the chapters. These two final strategies are not specific to fraction instruction. Instead, they are essential instructional techniques regardless of the content you are teaching. We feel, however, that they are particularly important to consider when helping students develop fraction sense because of the complexity of the topic and the many challenges students and teachers often face when it comes to the learning and teaching of fractions. We hope that you will find these to be valuable additions to your repertoire of teaching strategies.

Strategy #1: Provide opportunities for students to work with irregularly partitioned, and unpartitioned, areas, lengths, and number lines.

By providing opportunities for students to create partitions and reason about unequally partitioned shapes, you can help them develop a deep and flexible understanding of part–whole relations. As we discuss in Chapter 1, these kinds of experiences can help students move beyond a shallow understanding of part–whole relations that is based on merely counting parts to one that is based on truly understanding the relationship between the shaded part and

Ten Essential Strategies for Supporting Fraction Sense

1. Provide opportunities for students to work with irregularly partitioned, and unpartitioned, areas, lengths, and number lines. (Chapter 1)

2. Provide opportunities for students to investigate, assess, and refine mathematical "rules" and generalizations. (Chapter 2)

3. Provide opportunities for students to recognize equivalent fractions as different ways to name the same quantity. (Chapter 3)

4. Provide opportunities for students to work with changing units. (Chapter 4)

5. Provide opportunities for students to develop their understanding of the importance of context in fraction comparison tasks. (Chapter 5)

6. Provide meaningful opportunities for students to translate between fraction and decimal notation. (Chapter 6)

7. Provide opportunities for students to translate between different fraction representations. (Chapter 7)

8. Provide students with multiple strategies for comparing and reasoning about fractions. (Chapter 8)

9. Provide opportunities for students to engage in mathematical discourse and share and discuss their mathematical ideas, even those that may not be fully formed or completely accurate.

10. Provide opportunities for students to build on their reasoning and sense-making skills about fractions by working with a variety of manipulatives and tools, such as Cuisenaire rods, Pattern Blocks, Fraction Kits, and ordinary items from their lives.

the whole, the distance from 0 in relation to the unit distance on a number line, or the relationship between rods of different lengths.

Strategy #2: Provide opportunities for students to investigate, assess, and refine mathematical "rules" and generalizations.

It is not uncommon for children to misapply generalizations as they attempt to make sense of new and complex material. Helping them question and refine generalizations and strategies is extremely important in supporting students' development as mathematical sense-makers. In Chapter 2, we describe some activities you can use in your classroom.

Strategy #3: Provide opportunities for students to recognize equivalent fractions as different ways to name the same quantity.

Students should understand that equivalent fractions—such as $\frac{8}{12}$, $\frac{4}{6}$, and $\frac{2}{3}$—represent precisely the same point on the number line, and the differences in notation (how the fractions are written) are merely a matter of the value of the denominator. As we describe in Chapter 3, students often do not understand that equivalent fractions are multiple ways to name one quantity.

Strategy #4: Provide opportunities for students to work with changing units.

We need to help students understand that an object such as a triangle pattern block can be one-third of one thing (a trapezoid) and one-sixth of another (a hexagon). Activities like the ones we describe Chapter 4, which use materials such as Cuisenaire rods and Pattern Blocks and designate different items as the whole (or unit) can support students' understanding that a fraction is not a name for a given block but a relationship between the block and the whole.

Strategy #5: Provide opportunities for students to develop their understanding of the importance of context in fraction comparison tasks.

Fractions are representations of quantities, and these quantities are measured in relation to a unit (or a whole). The meaning of $\frac{2}{3}$ is determined in part by the size of the unit. As we describe in Chapter 5, students need opportunities to think about the importance of context in fraction comparison problems.

Strategy #6: Provide meaningful opportunities for students to translate between fraction and decimal notation.

Fraction and decimal notation are two different notational systems for rational numbers. Frequently, students do not see that a fraction and a decimal are merely two different ways to name a quantity. As we describe in Chapter 6, providing students with opportunities to work simultaneously with fraction and decimal notations supports their development of fraction sense.

Strategy #7: Provide opportunities for students to translate between different fraction representations.

In the elementary grades, students are introduced to multiple representations for fractions, including shaded parts of areas, parts of sets, and points on the number line. In Chapter 7 we discuss the importance of asking students to translate between different fraction representations. When students translate, they are forced to consider the features of the representation that are representation-specific, as well as those that have mathematical meaning beyond the representation.

Strategy #8: Provide students with multiple strategies for comparing and reasoning about fractions.

Students often rely on a common denominator strategy for comparing fractions, even when other strategies are more convenient or efficient. As we describe in Chapter 8, you can support your students in deepening their fraction sense by providing opportunities for them to use benchmarks to reason about fraction value, and by focusing their attention on the *relationships between* numerators and denominators (not just numerators *or* denominators).

Strategy #9: Provide opportunities for students to engage in mathematical discourse and share and discuss their mathematical ideas, even those that may not be fully formed or completely accurate.

In addition to providing opportunities for students to learn from their classmates, to refine their thinking by explaining to another person, and to use mathematical language in a meaningful way, classroom discussions can provide you with invaluable insights into what students do and do not understand about a given topic.

Strategy #10: Provide opportunities for students to build on their reasoning and sense-making skills about fractions by working with a variety of manipulatives and tools, such as Cuisenaire rods, Pattern Blocks, Fraction Kits, and ordinary items from their lives.

The more opportunities that students have to apply their fraction knowledge to solve problems involving different materials, contexts, settings, and relationships, the deeper and more flexible their understanding of fraction concepts will become.

Get Started!

The importance of helping students develop a deep and flexible understanding of foundational fraction concepts, such as those discussed in this book, cannot be overstated. The scenarios and research findings presented in the followings chapters illustrate many of the challenges students without fraction sense face as they attempt to solve fraction problems. By providing opportunities for your students to investigate, discuss, revise, expand, and refine their understanding of fractions, you can prepare them for success with fraction comparison and computation. This preparation will not only help them with fraction tasks they encounter in school, but it will also help them better appreciate and understand the important role fractions play in their world.

See Also

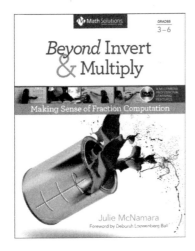

Beyond Invert & Multiply: Making Sense of Fraction Computation, Grades 3–6
A Multimedia Professional Learning Resource

This resource builds on the foundational understandings described in *Beyond Pizzas & Pies* and applies them to situations involving fraction computation. Throughout the resource connections are made to the "Ten Essential Strategies for Supporting Fraction Sense" previously listed.

A Letter from Math Coach Lori MacDonald

I cannot recall a time in my professional life when I've been more grateful for a resource. Teachers in Berkeley have been working hard learning the Common Core standards, paying special attention to the new emphasis on fractions. The standards seem logical, but we have many questions and some concerns as we enter our second year teaching them. Julie McNamara and Meghan Shaughnessy, in an immeasurably helpful way, have anticipated our situation and designed *Beyond Pizzas & Pies, Second Edition: 10 Essential Strategies for Supporting Fraction Sense* to lead us, step-by-important-step, into greater understanding of the standards and ways we might teach them effectively.

Many teachers are wondering, even after studying the standards carefully, "How am I supposed to teach something I don't yet fully understand?" My answer is, read *Beyond Pizzas & Pies*. Here's a quick look at how each section provides invaluable support.

Classroom Scenario

In the "Classroom Scenario" sections of *Beyond Pizzas & Pies*, the authors get right inside our heads. Through their deft analysis of teachers' thinking process, Julie and Meghan assure the reader that they understand our need to be led through a guided process to gain greater understanding. If we could have mastered the standards in one reading, we would have. Julie and Meghan begin each chapter with us in the classroom as we struggle with knowing how best to teach these unfamiliar concepts.

What's the Math?

The authors then begin a short but effective section of direction instruction, "What's the Math?," and we are listening, because we know Julie and Meghan get it. Having then acquired a better understanding of the concept at hand, we are pushed to consider what the research says. *Where are the typical misunderstandings among students? Among teachers? What has been shown to be most effective in terms of framing the concept?*

Classroom Activities

Then, once our trust has been earned and our understanding increased, right about the time we're thinking, "This is great, but I don't have time to translate this into lessons," *Beyond Pizzas & Pies* gives us "Classroom Activities," replete with reproducibles and video clips demonstrating how to teach the concept.

Wrapping It Up

In "Wrapping It Up," we are asked questions that show us how far we've come and challenge us to set concrete goals for implementing what we've learned.

Throughout the book, the reader feels as if she has a personal math guide. This is not an academic book, simply offering some good ideas on how you might approach teaching fractions. It is a systematic walk through of the Common Core State Standards for Mathematics. In the middle of explaining a new approach taken in the CCSSM, the authors remind us of how previous standards addressed similar concepts. By reminding us of how we previously understood (and probably taught) various concepts, our learning of the new standards is greatly facilitated. No ideas in this book are offered in a vacuum; Julie and Meghan create a context for all they discuss.

What a gift *Beyond Pizzas & Pies* is to teachers. Personal. Practical. Professional. I want every teacher and coach in Berkeley Unified to have a copy of this resource and to wear it out: mark it, bend its spine, and mine it for all its riches and classroom videos.

—Lori MacDonald, Coach, K–5 mathematics
Berkeley Unified School District, California

Summary of Connections with the Common Core State Standards

The following connections are also featured at the beginning of each of the corresponding chapters; they are included here as well for quick reference.

Chapter	CCSS Content Standards: Number and Operations: Fractions (NF); Geometry (G)
1	**Grade 3** **Number & Operations—Fractions** *Develop understanding of fractions as numbers.* **3NF.A.1:** Understand a fraction 1/b as the quantity formed by 1 part when a whole is partitioned into b equal parts; understand a fraction a/b as the quantity formed by a parts of size 1/b. **3NF.A.2:** Understand a fraction as a number on the number line; represent fractions on a number line diagram. **Geometry** Reason with shapes and their attributes. **3.G.A.2:** Partition shapes into parts with equal areas. Express the area of each part as a unit fraction of the whole.
2	**Grade 4** **Number & Operations—Fractions** *Extend understanding of fraction equivalence and ordering.* **4.NF.A.1:** Explain why a fraction a/b is equivalent to a fraction $(n \times a)/(n \times b)$ by using visual models, with attention to how the number and size of the parts differ even though the two fractions themselves are the same size. Use this principle to recognize and generate equivalent fractions. **4.NF.A.2:** Compare two fractions with different numerators and different denominators, e.g., by creating common denominators or numerators, or by comparing to a benchmark such as $\frac{1}{2}$. Recognize that comparisons are valid only when the two fractions refer to the same whole. Record the results of comparisons with symbols <, =, or <, and justify the conclusions, e.g., by using a visual fraction model.

(continued)

Chapter	CCSS Content Standards: Number and Operations: Fractions (NF); Geometry (G)
3	**Grade 3** **Number and Operations—Fractions** *Develop understanding of fractions as numbers.* **3.NF.A.3:** Explain equivalence of fractions in special cases, and compare fractions by reasoning about their size. **Grade 4** **Number and Operations—Fractions** *Extend understanding of fraction equivalence and ordering.* **4.NF.A.1:** Explain why a fraction a/b is equivalent to a fraction $(n \times a)/(n \times b)$ by using visual models, with attention to how the number and size of the parts differ even though the two fractions themselves are the same size. Use this principle to recognize and generate equivalent fractions. **4.NF.A.2:** Compare two fractions with different numerators and different denominators, e.g., by creating common denominators or numerators, or by comparing to a benchmark such as $\frac{1}{2}$. Recognize that comparisons are valid only when the two fractions refer to the same whole. Record the results of comparisons with symbols >, =, or <, and justify the conclusions, e.g., by using a visual fraction model. **Grade 5** **Number and Operations—Fractions** *Use equivalent fractions as a strategy to add and subtract fractions.* **5.NF.A.1:** Add and subtract fractions with unlike denominators (including mixed numbers) by replacing given fractions with equivalent fractions in such a way as to produce an equivalent sum or difference of fractions with like denominators. **5.NF.A.2:** Solve word problems involving addition and subtraction of fractions referring to the same whole, including cases of unlike denominators, e.g., by using visual fractions models or equations to represent the problem. Use benchmark fractions and number sense of fractions to estimate mentally and assess the reasonableness of answers.
4	**Grade 3** **Number and Operations—Fractions** *Develop understanding of fractions as numbers.* **3.NF.A.1:** Understand a fraction 1/b as the quantity formed by 1 part when a whole is partitioned into b equal parts; understand a fraction a/b as the quantity formed by a parts of size 1/b. **Geometry** *Reason with shapes and their attributes.* **3.GA.2:** Partition shapes into parts with equal areas. Express the area of each part as a unit fraction of the whole. **Grade 4** **Number and Operations—Fractions** *Extend understanding of fraction equivalence and ordering.* **4.NF.1:** Explain why a fraction a/b is equivalent to a fraction $(n \times a)/(n \times b)$ by using visual fraction models, with attention to how the number and size of the parts differ even though the two fractions themselves are the same size. Use this principle to recognize and generate equivalent fractions.

Chapter	CCSS Content Standards: Number and Operations: Fractions (NF); Geometry (G)
5	**Grade 3** **Number and Operations—Fractions** *Develop understanding of fractions as numbers.* **3.NF.A.1:** Understand a fraction 1/b as the quantity formed by 1 part when a whole is partitioned into b equal parts; understand a fraction a/b as the quantity formed by a parts of size 1/b. **3.NF.A.3:** Explain equivalence of fractions in special cases, and compare fractions by reasoning about their size. **3.NF.A.3.D:** Compare two fractions with the same numerator or the same denominator by reasoning about their size. Recognize that comparisons are valid only when the two fractions refer to the same whole. Record the results of comparisons with the symbols >, =, or <, and justify the conclusions, e.g., by using a visual fraction model.
6	**Grade 4** **Number and Operations—Fractions** *Understand decimal notation for fractions, and compare decimal fractions.* **4.NF.C.6:** Use decimal notation for fractions with denominators 10 or 100. **4.NF.C.7:** Compare two decimals to hundredths by reasoning about their size. Recognize that comparisons are valid only when the two decimals refer to the same whole. Record the results of the comparisons with the symbols >, =, or <, and justify the conclusions, e.g., by using a visual model. **Grade 5** **Number and Operations—Fractions** *Apply and extend previous understandings of multiplication and division.* **5.NF.B.3:** Interpret a fraction as division of the numerator by the denominator (a/b = a ÷ b). Solve word problems involving division of whole numbers leading to answers in the form of fractions or mixed numbers, e.g., by using visual fraction models or equations to represent the problem.

Chapter	CCSS Content Standards: Number and Operations: Fractions (NF); Geometry (G)
7	**Grade 3** **Number and Operations—Fractions** *Develop understanding of fractions as numbers.* **3.NF.A.2:** Understand a fraction as a number on the number line; represent fractions on a number line diagram. **Grade 4** **Number and Operations—Fractions** *Build fractions from unit fractions.* **4.NF.B.3:** Understand a fraction a/b with a > 1 as a sum of fractions 1/b. **4.NF.B.3.A:** Understand addition and subtraction of fractions as joining and separating parts referring to the same whole. **4.NF.B.3.D:** Solve word problems involving addition and subtraction of fractions referring to the same whole and having like denominators. **Grade 5** **Number and Operations—Fractions** *Use equivalent fractions as a strategy to add and subtract fractions.* **5.NF.A.2:** Solve word problems involving addition and subtraction of fractions referring to the same whole, including cases of unlike denominators.
8	**Grade 3** **Number and Operations—Fractions** *Develop understanding of fractions as numbers.* **3.NF.A.3:** Explain equivalence of fractions in special cases, and compare fractions by reasoning about their size. **Grade 4** **Number and Operations—Fractions** *Extend understanding of fraction equivalence and ordering.* **4.NF.A.1:** Explain why a fraction a/b is equivalent to a fraction n x a n x b by using visual fraction models, with attention to how the number and size of the parts differ even though the two fractions themselves are the same size. Use this principle to recognize and generate equivalent fractions. **4.NF.A.2:** Compare two fractions with different numerators and different denominators, e.g., by creating common denominators or numerators, or by comparing to a benchmark such as $\frac{1}{2}$. Recognize that comparisons are valid only when the two fractions refer to the same whole. Record the results of comparisons with symbols >, =, or <, and justify the conclusions, e.g., by using a visual fraction model.

Video Clips by Chapter

Page Number	Video Clip	Length	Title	Grade/Teacher
Chapter 1				
25	2a	1:17	Introducing Activity 2.1: Number Line Activities with Cuisenaire Rods	Grade 3/Mr. Seay
26	2b	1:40	Splitting the Number Line in Half	Grade 4/Ms. Lee
27	2c	2:03	The Purple Ones Work!	Grade 4/Ms. Lee
27	2d	:45	Lizette's Strategy for Finding the Rod That Is $\frac{1}{3}$ of the Unit Interval	Grade 4/Ms. Lee
28	2e	2:51	Labeling the Number Line	Grade 3/Mr. Seay
29	2f	1:09	Using Knowledge of $\frac{1}{2}$ to Find $\frac{1}{6}$s	Grade 4/Ms. Lee
30	2g	1:49	What Do You Know About Numbers Between 0 and 1?	Grade 3/Mr. Seay
31	2h	:38	What Are We Learning About Numbers Between 0 and 1?	Grade 3/Mr. Seay
32	2i	2:18	Revisiting the Question, "What Are the Numbers Between 0 and 1?"	Grade 3/Mr. Seay
Chapter 3				
50	3a	2:19	Introducing Activity 3.1: Measuring with Cuisenaire Rods	Grade 4/Ms. Thompson
51	3b	1:54	"How Many Brown Rods Long Is the Marker?"	Grade 4/Ms. Thompson
51	3c	:57	Different Names for the Remainder Length	Grade 4/Ms. Thompson
54	3d	:35	What Do We Call Four White Rods?	Grade 4/Ms. Thompson
54	3e	2:05	Making Monica's Thinking Public	Grade 4/Ms. Thompson
55	3f	1:45	Using the Rods to Show How $\frac{1}{2}$, $\frac{2}{4}$, and $\frac{4}{8}$ Are Equivalent	Grade 4/Ms. Thompson

(continued)

Video Clips by Chapter (cont'd)

Page Number	Video Clip	Length	Title	Grade/Teacher
Chapter 5				
86	5a	1:28	Reviewing the Names of the Pattern Blocks	Grade 3/Ms. McNamara
87	5b	3:06	Introducing Activity 5.1: Pattern Block Fractions, Version 2	Grade 3/Ms. McNamara
88	5c	2:22	What Do You Call the Triangle When the Trapezoid Is the Whole?	Grade 3/Ms. McNamara
88	5d	:58	Stephanie's Use of the Pattern Blocks to Support Her Reasoning	Grade 3/Ms. McNamara
90	5e	5:13	What Do You Call the Rhombus When the Trapezoid Is the Whole?	Grade 3/Ms. McNamara
91	5f	1:01	Is $\frac{1}{2}$ Always Greater Than $\frac{1}{3}$?	Grade 3/Ms. McNamara
Chapter 8				
134	8a	:52	Introducing Activity 8.1: More or Less Than $\frac{1}{2}$?	Grade 5/Ms. Kretschmar
135	8b	2:00	Labeling the Number Line	Grade 5/Ms. Kretschmar
137	8c	4:38	Fractions That Equal $\frac{1}{2}$	Grade 5/Ms. Kretschmar
137	8d	4:57	Describing the Relationship Between the Numerator and Denominator in Fractions Equal To $\frac{1}{2}$	Grade 5/Ms. Kretschmar and Ms. McNamara
138	8e	2:19	Reasoning About Fractions Less Than $\frac{1}{2}$	Grade 5/Ms. Kretschmar
139	8f	1:47	Using Academic Language to Describe the Relationship Between the Numerator and Denominator in Fractions Less Than $\frac{1}{2}$	Grade 5/Ms. Kretschmar
139	8g	4:03	Reasoning About Fractions Greater Than $\frac{1}{2}$	Grade 5/Ms. Kretschmar
140	8h	3:48	Reasoning About Fractions That Are Equal To, Less Than, and Greater Than $\frac{1}{2}$	Grade 5/Ms. Kretschmar

Video Clips by Grade, Including Demographics

Demographics: *The student body at Lighthouse Community Charter School comprises 81 percent Hispanic, 9 percent African American, 5 percent Multiethnic, 3 percent Asian/Pacific Islander, 1 percent Middle Eastern, and 1 percent Caucasian. Eight-one percent of students are English learners. Eight-six percent of the students receive free or reduced price lunch.*

Grade	Teacher	Video Clips
Grades 3, 5	Julie McNamara is the coauthor of *Beyond Pizzas & Pies, Second Edition*, and is thrilled to be a guest teacher in Ms. Hofmayer's class. She is sure she learned far more from the students than they learned from her!	5a Reviewing the Names of the Pattern Blocks 5b Introducing Activity 5.1: Pattern Block Fractions, Version 2 5c What Do You Call the Triangle When the Trapezoid Is the Whole? 5d Stephanie's Use of the Pattern Blocks to Support Her Reasoning 5e What Do You Call the Rhombus When the Trapezoid Is the Whole? 5f Is $\frac{1}{2}$ Always Greater Than $\frac{1}{3}$?
Grade 3	Mr. Seay previously taught third and fourth grade and has been teaching for more than ten years. He is currently the K–4 Academic Intervention Specialist at Lighthouse Community Charter School. He enjoys helping students build a strong foundation in mathematics and helping them critique each other's reasoning.	2a Introducing Activity 2.1: Number Line Activities with Cuisenaire Rods 2e Labeling the Number Line 2g What Do You Know About Numbers Between 0 and 1? 2h What Are We Learning About Numbers Between 0 and 1? 2i Revisiting the Question, "What Are the Numbers Between 0 and 1?"
Grade 4	Ms. Lee teaches third and fourth grade. She has been teaching for ten years, and has previously taught first and second grades as well. Ms. Lee places a high priority on student-led discussions and emphasizing multiple ways of problem solving in her teaching.	2b Splitting the Number Line in Half 2c The Purple Ones Work! 2d Lizette's Strategy for Finding the Rod That Is $\frac{1}{3}$ of the Unit Interval 2f Using Knowledge of $\frac{1}{2}$ to Find $\frac{1}{6}$s

(continued)

Grade	Teacher	Video Clips
Grade 4	Ms. Thompson has been teaching kindergarten through fourth grade for sixteen years. She currently teaches third and fourth grade. She is National Board Certified in Early/Middle Childhood Literacy, and is the leader of her school's third through sixth grade math inquiry group. She believes that encouraging and supporting children to make meaning is the foundation of good instruction in every content area.	3a Introducing Activity 3.1: Measuring with Cuisenaire Rods 3b "How Many Brown Rods Long Is the Marker?" 3c Different Names for the Remainder Length 3d What Do We Call Four White Rods? 3e Making Monica's Thinking Public 3f Using the Rods to Show How $\frac{1}{2}$, $\frac{2}{4}$, and $\frac{4}{8}$ Are Equivalent
Grade 5	Ms. Kretschmar teaches fifth- and sixth-grade math and science. She has been teaching and learning from her students for seventeen years. She puts a high priority on looking deeply at student work and listening to student thinking to inform instruction.	8a Introducing Activity 8.1: More or Less Than $\frac{1}{2}$? 8b Labeling the Number Line 8c Fractions That Equal $\frac{1}{2}$ 8d Describing the Relationship Between the Numerator and Denominator in Fractions Equal To $\frac{1}{2}$ 8e Reasoning About Fractions Less Than $\frac{1}{2}$ 8f Using Academic Language to Describe the Relationship Between the Numerator and Denominator in Fractions Less Than $\frac{1}{2}$ 8g Reasoning About Fractions Greater Than $\frac{1}{2}$ 8h Reasoning About Fractions That Are Equal To, Less Than, and Greater Than $\frac{1}{2}$

The Problem with Partitioning

It's Not Just About Counting the Pieces

Strategy #1

Provide opportunities for students to work with irregularly partitioned, and unpartitioned, areas, lengths, and number lines.

CCSS Connections

Grade 3

Number & Operations—Fractions

Develop understanding of fractions as numbers.

3NF.A.1: Understand a fraction $1/b$ as the quantity formed by 1 part when a whole is partitioned into b equal parts; understand a fraction a/b as the quantity formed by a parts of size $1/b$.

3NF.A.2: Understand a fraction as a number on the number line; represent fractions on a number line diagram.

Geometry

Reason with shapes and their attributes.

3.G.A.2: Partition shapes into parts with equal areas. Express the area of each part as a unit fraction of the whole.

Mr. Burnett thought his third graders really understood how to name fractions of areas because most of the children were able to provide correct answers to problems like this:

Write a fraction to show how much of the large square is shaded.

He was pleased that many students could also explain how they arrived at their answer. The children told him that they first counted the number of parts the square was divided into (4) and used that number for the denominator. Then, they counted the number of shaded parts (1) and used that number for the numerator.

Before moving on, however, Mr. Burnett decided to show his students a slightly different version of the same problem, one that he had encountered at a teachers' conference the previous year:

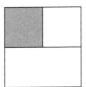

Write a fraction to show how much of the large square is shaded.

He was shocked by their responses! Many students wrote $\frac{1}{3}$ for the second problem, even though most had written $\frac{1}{4}$ for the first problem. Mr. Burnett decided to ask a few students how they came up with $\frac{1}{3}$. Maya said, "First I counted the total number of parts (three) and put that as the denominator. Then I counted the number of shaded parts (one) and used that for the numerator."

Luc said, "It's just like the other one, only this time it's one out of three instead of one out of four."

Mr. Burnett sighed, because he realized his students were following the procedure he had taught them: counting parts. He knew he needed to address this issue, but he wasn't quite sure what to do.

Representing a fractional part of an area using fraction notation involves determining the whole and then considering the size of the shaded part of the area in relation to the size of the whole. According to the Common Core State Standards for Mathematics (2010), students in grade 3 need to "understand a fraction 1/b as the quantity formed by 1 part when a whole is partitioned into b equal parts." In the following illustration, the whole is the large square. There are different strategies for thinking about the size of the part of the area that is shaded gray in relation to the whole (the large square).

Part–Whole Strategy

One strategy involves dividing (partitioning) the whole into parts of equal size. In the next illustration, for example, the whole is divided (partitioned) into four equal parts (the denominator) by inserting the dotted line, and one of these parts is shaded gray (the numerator). The shaded part of the area can be called $\frac{1}{4}$. This corresponds to the partitive meaning of $1 \div 4$.

Measurement Strategy

A second strategy for considering the size of the shaded part in relation to the whole entails considering the number of copies of the shaded part needed to cover the whole. This is the denominator. As shown in the next illustration, it takes four copies of the shaded part to cover the whole. In the original task, one of these copies is shaded (the numerator), and thus we can represent the size of the shaded part of the whole as $\frac{1}{4}$:

Students come to formal fractions instruction with a history of formal and informal experiences in working with whole numbers. Through these experiences, students have learned many principles and procedures for working with whole numbers. For example, they have learned that when they multiply two whole numbers, the product is always equal to (as in the case of 1×8) or greater than (as in the case of 2×8) at least one of the factors. Students often find fractions challenging because the principles and procedures for working with fractions differ in important ways from the principles and procedures for working with whole numbers.

Researchers note that students often extend their knowledge of whole numbers to think about fractions in inappropriate ways. Nancy Mack, a professor at Grand Valley State University, conducted several teaching studies with children to investigate their understanding of fractions and how they solve fraction problems. She found that students often use knowledge and strategies that make sense in the context of problems involving whole numbers to solve problems involving fractions. As a result, students may not attend to the relationship between parts and wholes when they provide a fractional name for part of a shaded square. Instead, they just count the parts. In addition, Mack found that it is quite common for students to use both whole numbers and fractions to represent the same fractional quantity. For example, a student named Todd told her, "I can write five eighths as five or . . . five eighths. It doesn't matter. It's the same thing" (1995, 437).

Geoffrey Saxe, Edward Taylor, Clifton McIntosh, and Maryl Gearhart, professors and researchers at the University of California, Berkeley, found that it is not uncommon for upper elementary school students to respond to fraction tasks by counting the parts, as Mr. Burnett's students did. In a study published in 2005, they examined students' representations of shaded parts of an area as fraction notations using both equally and unequally partitioned shapes. They found that although 69 percent of upper elementary school students appropriately represented shaded parts of an area that were equally partitioned, only 9 percent of students appropriately interpreted shaded parts of an area that were unequally partitioned. Many of the students who gave the correct fraction notation for the equally partitioned area may have been focusing on the number of parts in relation to the total number of parts without considering the *size* of those parts.

The students' focus on counts of parts without consideration of size is not specific to shaded parts of an area. The same issues arise when students try similar tasks that involve number lines. With number lines, students tend to focus on the number of tick marks or the number of segments into which the unit distance is divided. They ignore the distance of the segments, and they do not focus on the directed distance of the point from 0 in relation to a unit distance (Bright, Behr, Post, and Wachsmuth 1988; Saxe, Shaughnessy, Shannon, Langer-Osuna, Chinn, and Gearhart 2007). For instance, students might label the point marked on the following number line as $\frac{3}{5}$ because the unit (the interval from 0 to 1) is divided into five segments and the point is located at the end of the third segment, even though the length of the segments is not equal:

This research highlights the difficulties students often face when instruction in fractions does not provide opportunities for them to develop their understanding beyond a very limited view of part–whole relations. Like Luc, they may think, "It's just like the other one, only this time it's one out of three instead of one out of four." The following classroom activities will help students understand part–whole relations as a proportional relationship, not merely a counting exercise. The activities all emphasize the importance of the size of the part in relation to the whole.

1.1   Given the Fraction, Draw the Partitions

Overview

In this activity, students partition a variety of shapes and number lines to show a specified fraction. Students also identify shaded parts of area and points on the number line. Some of the representations are partitioned equally and others are not. Together, these activities provide opportunities for students to reason about the meaning of part–whole relations.

<table>
<tr><th colspan="2">Materials</th></tr>
<tr><td>predrawn shapes and number lines (create your own or use Reproducibles 1a and 1b)</td></tr>
</table>

1. Provide students with several different shapes and number lines and ask them to show or shade a particular fractional part. We have included some examples to help you get started, but you can use any shape and any fraction. This task can be easily differentiated by providing students with areas that are more or less straightforward to partition. (See Figure 1–1; also available as Reproducibles 1a and 1b.)

 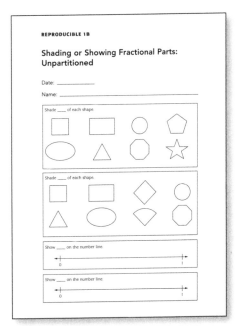

Figure 1–1. Shading or Showing Fractional Parts: Unpartitioned (Reproducibles 1a and 1b)

2. After students have partitioned their shapes and number lines, ask several students to share their solutions. Make sure that they justify their partitioning and explain their thinking to the class. Ask students to compare the different ways that the shapes have been shaded to help them understand that there are different ways to shade a fraction of a shape. For example, students may shade half of the square in the following ways, all of which correctly represent the value of half of the square:

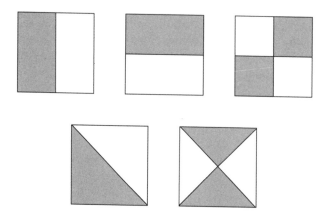

ASSESSMENT OPPORTUNITY

Students' solutions, both correct and incorrect, can lead to very fruitful conversations in terms of both learning opportunities for students and assessment opportunities for you. For example, it is not uncommon for students to be able to divide circles fairly accurately to show $\frac{1}{2}$s by drawing a vertical line right down the center of the circle.

When asked to show $\frac{1}{4}$s, these same students may again draw vertical lines so that the circle is not equally partitioned. This can lead to a very rich discussion about what to call the parts. Are they $\frac{1}{4}$s or something else? Are all the parts the same size? Does this matter? What would need to be true about the four parts in order for them to be $\frac{1}{4}$s?

Common partitioning to show $\frac{1}{2}$

Common partitioning to show $\frac{1}{4}$

3. Provide opportunities for students to work with prepartitioned areas and number lines in which the number of partitions does not correspond to the denominator of the fraction. (See Figure 1–2; also available as Reproducible 1c.) Again, ensure that students provide a rationale for their work and that they share their ideas with the class.

4. Finally, provide opportunities for students to work with unequally partitioned areas and number lines like the one that stumped Mr. Burnett's class, and ask them to name the shaded portion/point on the number line. (See Figure 1–3; also available as Reproducible 1d.) Activities like this provide prime opportunities to discuss what it really means for something to be a fraction of something else. In the example of the unequally partitioned square, encourage students to think in terms of how many of the smaller shaded squares it would take to cover the larger square. This is a much more precise and mathematically accurate way to help students develop their understanding of part–whole relations than simply having them count parts.

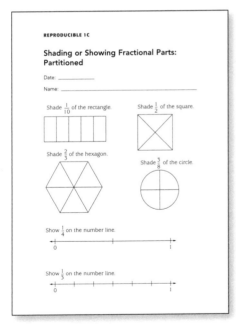

Figure 1–2. Shading or Showing Fractional Parts: Partitioned (Reproducible 1c)

Figure 1–3. Shading or Showing Fractional Parts: Unequally Partitioned (Reproducible 1d)

1.2 Part to Whole and Whole to Part

Overview

By using different-length rods as the part and the whole, students develop their understanding that fractions such as $\frac{1}{2}$ or $\frac{3}{4}$ are not names for specific rods, but rather descriptions of relationships between the rod designated as the part and the rod length designated as the whole.

Materials

Fractions with Cuisenaire Rods recording sheet, 1 copy per student (**Reproducible 1e**)

Cuisenaire rods, 1 set per pair of students

1. Pass out the materials. (See Figure 1–4; also available as Reproducible 1e.) Instruct students to take out the 10-cm orange rod. Hold up the orange rod and ask, "Which rod is equal to one-half of this one?"

Most students will have no trouble identifying the 5-cm yellow rod as half of the orange rod. Ask students to explain why they chose the yellow rod, and what they notice about how many yellow rods are the same length as the orange rod and the fraction $\frac{1}{2}$. Use questioning to help students come to see the relationship between the number of yellows (two) that are the same length as one orange and the fraction $\frac{1}{2}$. Have a student name this

---

REPRODUCIBLE 1E

Part to Whole and Whole to Part

Date: _____

Name: _____

1. Start with the orange rod.
   a. Which rod is $\frac{1}{2}$ of the orange rod? _____
      How do you know?

   b. Which rod is $\frac{1}{5}$ of the orange rod? _____
      How do you know?

   c. Which rod is $\frac{1}{10}$ of the orange rod? _____
      How do you know?

2. Take out the brown rod.
   a. Which rod is $\frac{1}{2}$ of the brown rod? _____
      How do you know?

   b. Which rod is $\frac{1}{4}$ of the brown rod? _____
      How do you know?

   c. Which rod is $\frac{1}{8}$ of the brown rod? _____
      How do you know?

REPRODUCIBLE 1E (cont'd)

3. Take out the light-green rod.
   a. If the light-green rod is $\frac{1}{3}$, which rod is the whole?
      _____
      How do you know?

   b. If the light-green rod is $\frac{1}{3}$, which rod is $\frac{2}{3}$?
      _____
      How do you know?

4. Take out the white rod.
   a. If the white rod is $\frac{1}{3}$, which rod is the whole?
      _____
      How do you know?

   b. If the white rod is $\frac{1}{3}$, which rod is $\frac{2}{3}$? _____
      How do you know?

5. Take out the dark-green rod.
   a. If the dark-green rod is $\frac{3}{4}$, which rod is the whole?
      _____
      How do you know?

   b. If the dark-green rod is $\frac{3}{4}$, which rod is the whole?
      _____
      How do you know?

Figure 1–4. Part to Whole and Whole to Part (Reproducible 1e) relationship in words by saying something like, "It takes two yellow rods to be the same length as one orange rod, so one yellow rod is $\frac{1}{2}$ of the orange rod." It's not important yet that all students completely understand the reciprocal relationship between $\frac{1}{2}$ and 2, but if some students indicate that they think there is something interesting about the numbers, ask them to explain and suggest that they keep their theory or conjecture in mind as you continue to explore with the Cuisenaire rods.

Manipulative Note

Cuisenaire rods are wooden or plastic blocks that range in length from 1 to 10 cm. Each rod of a given length is the same color. That is, all the 1-cm rods are white, all the 2-cm rods are red, all the 3-cm rods are light green, and so on.

Manipulative Note

The 1-cm Cuisenaire rod may be either white or tan, depending on the set

2. Next, ask students to find the rod that is $\frac{1}{5}$ of the orange rod. This will typically be more challenging than finding the rod that is $\frac{1}{2}$ of the orange rod. You can guide students by reminding them that there was something interesting between the number of yellow rods (two) that were the same length as one orange rod and the denominator of the fraction $\frac{1}{2}$.

3. After students have found that the 2-cm red rod is $\frac{1}{5}$ of the orange rod, ask them to find the rod that is $\frac{1}{10}$ of the orange rod. Then, ask the class to begin making some conjectures about the relationships they are finding.

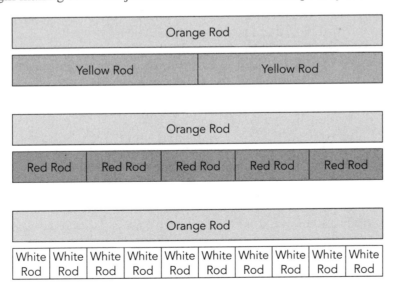

To make the relationship between the number of rods and the fractional value of one rod more explicit, have students begin a chart like the one shown here.

Whole: Orange Rod		
Part	How many to make the whole	Fraction name for part
Yellow	2	$\frac{1}{2}$, one-half
Red	5	$\frac{1}{5}$, one-fifth
White	10	$\frac{1}{10}$, one-tenth

4. After students have explored the relationship of all the rods to the orange rod, repeat the process using the 8-cm brown rod as the unit. When you ask, "Which rod is one-half of the brown rod?" some students may answer, "The yellow rod!" This is an indication that these students are not focusing on the relationships between the rods, but are instead thinking that the yellow rod is always $\frac{1}{2}$. Remind students of how they knew the yellow rod was $\frac{1}{2}$ of the orange rod—two yellows were the same length as one orange. Guide them to find the rod that has this same relationship with the brown rod.

5. Next ask, "Which rod is one-fourth of the brown rod?" Students may be confused to find that the rod that was called $\frac{1}{5}$ when the orange rod was the unit is now $\frac{1}{4}$ of the brown rod. This is an excellent opportunity to make explicit the fact that a fraction is a relationship between two quantities, and that knowing the whole (in this case, the rod) is extremely important when naming fractions.

By intentionally changing the rod that is used as the unit/whole, you are guiding students to the understanding that the label $\frac{1}{4}$ or $\frac{1}{5}$ is not just a name for the rod, but a description of the relationship between the red rod and whatever rod is being considered as the whole.

6. Finally, have students find $\frac{1}{8}$ of the brown rod. Continue to do this activity using different rods as the whole or starting point. When your students are comfortable with naming the rods in this way, ask them to work backward by showing a rod such as the 3-cm light-green rod and asking, "If this rod is one-third, which rod is the whole?" Even more challenging, show students a rod such as the 6-cm dark-green rod and ask, "If this rod is three-fourths, which rod is the whole?"

For More Information

All of the activities described in this chapter provide opportunities for students to develop a more flexible and mathematically sound understanding of part–whole relations than many of the more common activities found in curricular materials. Students need to be engaged in activities in which they

1. Encounter unusually partitioned areas and number lines

2. Design their own strategies for creating fractional parts of areas and number lines

3. Use materials such as Cuisenaire rods to work with changing unit sizes

In this way, we can help students move beyond simply counting parts to the understanding that "the size of a fractional part is relative to the size of the whole" (NCTM 2006, 15).

Study Questions

After Reading Chapter 1

1. What information presented in the "Classroom Scenario," "What's the Math?," and "What's the Research?" sections was familiar to you or similar to your experience with students?

2. What information presented in the "Classroom Scenario," "What's the Math?," and "What's the Research?" sections was new or surprising to you?

3. Which of the "Classroom Activities" (Activity 1.1: *Given the Fraction, Draw the Partitions*; Activity 1.2: *Part to Whole and Whole to Part*) do you plan to implement with your students?

After Trying One or More of the Activities

1. Describe the activity and any modifications you made to meet your students' needs and/or to align with your curriculum.

2. How did this activity add to your knowledge of what your students do and do not understand about fraction names and fraction notation?

3. What are your next steps for supporting your students' learning about fraction names and fraction notation?

Connections to *Beyond Invert & Multiply*

The foundational understandings introduced in *Beyond Pizzas & Pies* are further developed in its companion resource, *Beyond Invert & Multiply*. We recommend pairing this chapter with Chapter 1 in *Beyond Invert & Multiply* to further your learning.

Top or Bottom: Which One Matters?

Helping Students Reason About Generalizations Regarding Numerators and Denominators

Strategy #2
Provide opportunities for students to investigate, assess, and refine mathematical "rules" and generalizations.

CCSS Connections

Grade 4

Number & Operations—Fractions

Extend understanding of fraction equivalence and ordering.

4.NF.A.1: Explain why a fraction a/b is equivalent to a fraction $(n \times a)/(n \times b)$ by using visual models, with attention to how the number and size of the parts differ even though the two fractions themselves are the same size. Use this principle to recognize and generate equivalent fractions.

4.NF.A.2: Compare two fractions with different numerators and different denominators, e.g., by creating common denominators or numerators, or by comparing to a benchmark such as $\frac{1}{2}$. Recognize that comparisons are valid only when the two fractions refer to the same whole. Record the results of comparisons with symbols $<$, $=$, or $<$, and justify the conclusions, e.g., by using a visual fraction model.

In order to help her students understand the relative size of different fractions, Ms. Alvarez posed the following question: "Would you rather share your favorite pizza with three other people or seven other people? If the group ate the whole pizza, and everyone ate the same amount so they each got a fair share, which way would you get more: with three other people or seven other people? Work together in your group and make a poster showing your answer. Provide a clear explanation using pictures, numbers, and words."

Ms. Alvarez was very pleased by her students' posters and presentations. For the most part, the students' posters indicated that they would much rather share the pizza with three other people because that way they would get more pizza. (See Figure 2–1.)

We would much rather share with 3 people because we would get more pizza!

Size of pieces when you share with 3 people

Size of pieces when you share with 7 people

Figure 2–1. Poster Example

After reaching consensus that everyone would rather be in the group with four people than with eight, because having fewer people to share with would mean each person would get more pizza, Ms. Alvarez posed the following question: "So now I have a question for all of you. Which is bigger, one-fourth or one-eighth? Give me a thumbs-up if you think one-fourth is bigger, give me a thumbs sideways if you think one-eighth is bigger, and put your thumb on your nose if you're not sure."

Ms. Alvarez knew that this question would present a challenge for many students even though they all understood the sharing context. As she looked around her classroom she saw that although several students had their thumbs up, a fair number had them sideways or on their nose. Ms. Alvarez asked her students to discuss the question with their table groups and to try to come up with a generalization about fraction sizes in general.

"Well," Dominique began, "I think you could say that if the number of pieces the thing is cut into is smaller, the fraction is larger. And if the number of pieces the thing is cut into is larger, the fraction is smaller."

"Thank you, Dominique. Can someone restate Dominique's idea using the math word that means 'the number of pieces the thing is cut into'?" asked Ms. Alvarez.

Noticing Noah's hand, Ms. Alvarez called on him. "Here goes. The smaller the denominator, the larger the fraction. The larger the denominator, the smaller the fraction."

"What do you think about that?" Ms. Alvarez asked the class. Several students nodded enthusiastically and many gave Noah a thumbs-up. "Let's all say Noah's idea together: *The smaller the denominator, the larger the fraction. The larger the denominator, the smaller the fraction.*" Ms. Alvarez recorded Noah's conjecture while chanting along with the class, happy that they seemed to understand this important idea.

A few days later Ms. Alvarez was looking over the students' homework and was dismayed to see that in response to the prompt

Circle the larger fraction: $\frac{1}{2}$ $\frac{3}{4}$

many of them had indicated that $\frac{1}{2}$ was greater than $\frac{3}{4}$. When Ms. Alvarez asked Dominique to explain her answer during homework check, Dominique replied, "Remember, you taught us last week—the smaller the denominator, the larger the fraction. The larger the denominator, the smaller the fraction. Two is smaller than four, so one-half has got to be bigger than three-fourths."

As several students nodded their agreement with Dominique, Ms. Alvarez realized they had overgeneralized this important idea. She also realized her students were thinking only of the denominators of the fractions they were comparing, not realizing that in order to understand the value of a fraction they needed to consider both the numerator and denominator as well as their relationship to each other. Ms. Alvarez decided she would need to review this with her students and help them understand that both parts of a fraction are equally important.

When comparing fractions, students need to consider the size of the whole and interpret each fraction as a single number defined by the relationship between the numerator and the denominator.

Fractions can be compared in several different ways. Finding a common denominator or cross-multiplying to compare are two common approaches that students learn in school, but these approaches do not explicitly require a consideration of the size of the fractions. As Van de Walle, Karp, and Bay-Williams (2009) note, other strategies include:

- Same number of parts but parts of different sizes (same numerators);
- More and less than one-half or one whole; and
- Closeness to one-half or one whole.

These strategies support reasoning about the size of the fractions; however, the efficiency of each strategy varies based on the fractions involved. Here are examples of these and other comparison strategies:

Finding a Common Denominator (more of the same-size parts)

$$\frac{5}{6} \times \frac{4}{4} = \frac{20}{24}$$

$$\frac{7}{8} \times \frac{3}{3} = \frac{21}{24}$$

$$\frac{20}{24} < \frac{21}{24}, \text{ so } \frac{5}{6} < \frac{7}{8}$$

Cross-Multiplication (implicitly finding a common denominator)

$$\frac{5}{6} \diagup\!\!\!\!\diagdown \frac{7}{8} \qquad 5 \times 8 = 40 \qquad 6 \times 7 = 42$$

$$40 < 42, \text{ so } \frac{5}{6} < \frac{7}{8}$$

More of the Same-Size Parts

$$\frac{2}{3} > \frac{1}{3}$$

Same Number of Parts, But Parts of Different Sizes

Fourths are larger then eighths, so $\frac{3}{4} > \frac{3}{8}$

Closeness to One Whole

$\frac{7}{8}$ is $\frac{1}{8}$ less than 1. $\frac{5}{6}$ is $\frac{1}{6}$ less than 1. $\frac{1}{6}$ is greater than $\frac{1}{8}$, so $\frac{7}{8}$ is closer to 1.

$\frac{7}{8}$ is $\frac{1}{8}$ away from 1

$\frac{5}{6}$ is $\frac{1}{6}$ away from 1

Distance from 0

One can locate both numbers on a number line to determine distance from 0 (alternatively, a single number line could be used):

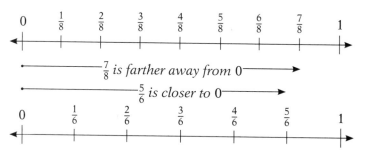

$\frac{7}{8}$ is farther away from 0

$\frac{5}{6}$ is closer to 0

Size of the Shaded Area

$\frac{7}{8} > \frac{5}{6}$

D uring spring 2009, we asked 267 fourth and sixth graders to respond to the following prompt:

Circle the larger fraction. $\frac{5}{6}$ $\frac{7}{8}$
Explain your answer.

We hoped that students would select $\frac{7}{8}$ and explain their answer using a variety of strategies such as the ones described in the "What's the Math?" section.

We were very surprised by the number of students who chose $\frac{5}{6}$ as the larger of the two fractions (40 percent of fourth graders and 34 percent of sixth graders). Even more surprising were the reasons students gave for *why* they circled $\frac{5}{6}$. A large percentage of the students who indicated that $\frac{5}{6}$ is larger than $\frac{7}{8}$ explained their answer by stating that "sixths are bigger than eighths," and many wrote a variation on "the smaller the denominator, the larger the fraction." For example, one fourth grader represented $\frac{5}{6}$ and $\frac{7}{8}$ using an area model (a circle) and explained that "if the denomonator [*sic*] is smaller the peice [*sic*] is bigger." (See Figure 2–2.)

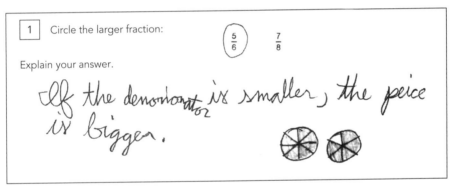

1   Circle the larger fraction: $\frac{5}{6}$ $\frac{7}{8}$

Explain your answer.

If the denomonator is smaller, the peice is bigger.

Figure 2–2. If the denominator is smaller, the piece is bigger.

We saw very similar responses among the sixth graders who chose $\frac{5}{6}$ as the larger fraction. For example, one student made a comparison in terms of the specific fractions included in the problem, sixths and eighths. (See Figure 2–3 on page 22.) Another sixth grader provided a more generalized rationale, that "the smaller the number the bigger the pieces." (See Figure 2–4 on page 22.)

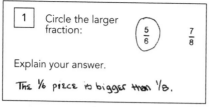

Explain your answer.

The 1/6 piece is bigger than 1/8.

Figure 2–3. The $\frac{1}{6}$ piece is bigger than $\frac{1}{8}$.

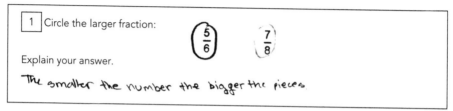

Explain your answer.

The smaller the number the bigger the pieces

Figure 2–4. The smaller the number the bigger the pieces.

This finding indicates that students may be responding to only one aspect of the written fraction—in this case, the denominator—instead of attending to both the numerator and denominator as necessary components of the number. This is like looking at a number such as 432, in which each of the digits provides crucial information about the value of the number, but the digits have to be considered in relation to each other to provide the whole story. If students focus only on the numerator or denominator, they are not considering the value of the fraction.

Even among students who circled the correct answer ($\frac{7}{8}$), some indicated that their reason for choosing $\frac{7}{8}$ was based on the value of the numerator only. (See Figure 2–5.)

Figure 2–5. This one is bigger because there are more pieces.

Still other students paid attention to both the numerators and denominators when comparing the fractions, but did not consider the relationship between them. For instance, a subset of students indicated that $\frac{7}{8}$ is the larger fraction because 7 is greater than 5 and 8 is greater than 6. (See Figure 2–6.)

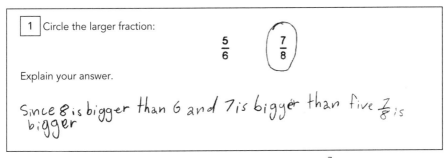

Figure 2–6. Since 8 is bigger than 6 and 7 is bigger than five, $\frac{7}{8}$ is bigger.

These types of responses present compelling evidence that many students are not attending to the relationship between numerators and denominators when asked to reason about fractional values and make comparisons between two or more fractions. This provides further confirmation of the claims made by Nancy Mack (2001), a professor at Grand Valley State University, that students often rely on whole number strategies when solving fraction problems.

When asked to compare two fractions such as $\frac{1}{2}$ and $\frac{3}{4}$, many of Ms. Alvarez's students had overgeneralized the important mathematical idea that fractions with smaller denominators are larger than those with larger denominators. What her students failed to realize was that this generalization, or "rule," had developed from a situation in which the numerators of both fractions were the same ($\frac{1}{4}$ versus $\frac{1}{6}$). When comparing $\frac{1}{2}$ and $\frac{3}{4}$, many students did not realize or remember that both the numerators and denominators of the fractions needed to be considered when comparing their values. When students overgeneralize in this manner, they may not be thinking of fractions as numbers, but only as groups of items or parts of shaded areas. The following classroom activities will help students increase their understanding of fractions as numbers and increase their ability to develop and apply appropriate generalizations.

2.1 Number Line Activities with Cuisenaire Rods, Version 1

Overview

In these activities, students use the number line to discover that the rule "the smaller the denominator, the larger the fraction" holds true only when the numerators are the same, because $\frac{1}{2}$ is indeed larger than $\frac{1}{4}$, and $\frac{1}{4}$ is larger than $\frac{1}{8}$. In addition, $\frac{2}{2}$ is larger than $\frac{2}{4}$, and $\frac{2}{4}$ is larger than $\frac{2}{8}$. Students can also see, however, that when the numerators are different, the comparison of any two fractions is more complex. Knowing the denominator of a fraction is a very important aspect of understanding its value, but it is only part of the information that is necessary. In much the same way, knowing only the numerator of a fraction is not sufficient when it comes to understanding the value.

Materials

12-cm Number Lines recording sheet, 1 copy per student **(Reproducible 2a)**

Cuisenaire rods, 1 set per pair of students

Manipulative Note

Cuisenaire rods are wooden or plastic blocks that range in length from 1 to 10 cm. Each rod of a given length is the same color. That is, all the 1-cm rods are white, all the 2-cm rods are red, all the 3-cm rods are light green, and so on.

1. Pass out the *12-cm Number Lines* recording sheets. (See Figure 2–7; also available as Reproducible 2a.) Using 12 cm as the unit interval allows students to use the rods to partition the unit into twelfths, sixths, fourths, thirds, and halves.

Figure 2–7. 12-cm Number Lines (Reproducible 2a)

2. Have students draw a bracket on the first number line to indicate that the distance from 0 to 1 is the unit interval. Instruct students to find the rod that allows them to partition the units on the first number line into halves. Have students use the 6-cm dark-green rod to mark $\frac{1}{2}$ on the number line:

Unit Interval

VIDEO CLIP 2a

Introducing Activity 2.1: Number Line Activities with Cuisenaire Rods

In this clip, which takes place at the beginning of Activity 2.1, we see the teacher, Mr. Seay, share something he observed in partner work: a "solution" for partitioning the unit interval on the number line in two parts. How does Mr. Seay's sharing of this observation help students' understanding?

For commentary on the above, see the Appendix: Authors' Video Reflections.

VIDEO CLIP 2b

Splitting the Number Line in Half

After partitioning the number line in half in Activity 2.1, two students in Ms. Lee's class share their thinking about how to partition the unit interval in half. What is the purpose of Ms. Lee's questioning?

For commentary on the above, see the Appendix: Authors' Video Reflections.

3. Next, have students find the rod that will enable them to partition the next number line in thirds:

VIDEO CLIP 2c

The Purple Ones Work!

In this clip, we see two students working on Step 3 of Activity 2.1: Find the rods that will partition the number line equally into $\frac{1}{3}$s. The students first try partitioning the unit interval into $\frac{1}{3}$s with the yellow rods because when they previously worked with a fraction kit, the yellow ones were the $\frac{1}{3}$s. How does the students' thinking change as they work to solve the problem? Why do the students decide that the purple rods, not the yellow rods, work? How do they come to this conclusion?

For commentary on the above, see the Appendix: Authors' Video Reflections.

VIDEO CLIP 2d

Lizette's Strategy for Finding the Rod That Is $\frac{1}{3}$ of the Unit Interval

In this clip from Activity 2.1, Ms. Lee asks Lizette to share how she partitioned the unit interval into $\frac{1}{3}$s. How does Lizette justify her use of the pink (purple) rods? What important idea, tied to the definition of a unit fraction, does Lizette draw on in her explanation?

For commentary on the above, see the Appendix: Authors' Video Reflections.

Labeling the Number Line

In this clip from Activity 2.1, we see Mr. Seay demonstrating for students how to label the number line after the unit interval has been partitioned into $\frac{1}{3}$s. How does Mr. Seay's explicit use of the chart and the large number line help students' understanding?

For commentary on the above, see the Appendix: Authors' Video Reflections.

4. Continue in this manner until students have partitioned and labeled the final three number lines into fourths, sixths, and twelfths:

VIDEO CLIP 2f

Using Knowledge of $\frac{1}{2}$ to find $\frac{1}{6}$s

In this clip, we see Marcela and Camilo describing how they found the rods that are $\frac{1}{6}$ of the unit interval. What important fraction concept does Marcela's reasoning support?

For commentary on the above, see the Appendix: Authors' Video Reflections.

5. After students have partitioned and labeled their number lines, ask for observations about the numbers they have written. It is important that you begin to refer to fractions as numbers, so that students become comfortable with this language as well.

> ### Teaching Note
>
> See Chapter 3 for further discussion of helping students understand fractions as numbers.

6. Pose one or more of the questions in the table on page 33 to help students reason about fractions as numbers.

2.2 Number Line Activities with Cuisenaire Rods, Version 2

Overview

Materials
large 0–1 number line
fraction kit or Cuisenaire rods

As students transition from using concrete materials like fraction kits and Cuisenaire rods to more abstract representations like number lines, they may need explicit support to begin considering fractions as numbers and not just names for pieces from their kits and different colored Cuisenaire rods. Activity 2.2 can be implemented as an opening and closing activity for many lessons focused on building foundational fraction concepts, including Activity 2.1. Before the lesson, this activity can provide you with invaluable assessment information regarding your students' familiarity with fractions as numbers. Afterward, it can provide closure for your students and help you determine where to go next.

1. Gather students together and display a number line like the one shown here.

2. Tell students you are going to talk about the numbers between 0 and 1 and ask them what they know about these numbers.

3. Take all suggestions and record them on or near the number line.

VIDEO CLIP 2g

What Do You Know About Numbers Between 0 and 1?

Before launching Activity 2.2, Mr. Seay asks his third graders to share what they think about the numbers between 0 and 1. What do students seem to know about these numbers?

For commentary on the above, see the Appendix: Authors' Video Reflections.

4. Have students complete Steps 1–5 of Activity 2.1: *Number Line Activities with Cuisenaire Rods,* in which they use Cuisenaire rods to partition number lines into halves, thirds, fourths, sixths, and twelfths.

5. After students have had time to explore with the materials, pause and refer them back to the number line. Ask them to share what they are learning about numbers between 0 and 1. You may need to explicitly tell them that the fractions they are exploring are actually numbers and each has a place on the number line.

VIDEO CLIP 2h

What Are We Learning About Numbers Between 0 and 1?

During Activity 2.2, Mr. Seay asks students if they are beginning to find numbers between 0 and 1. How do students respond? How does this activity support students' understanding of fractions?

For commentary on the above, see the Appendix: Authors' Video Reflections.

6. When students have completed the fraction exploration portion of the lesson, gather them together once again and revisit the number line and question from the beginning of the activity. Ask students to tell you the names of some of the numbers between 0 and 1. As students provide fractions, carefully partition the number line and place the fractions in the appropriate place on the line, again reinforcing that the fractions they are naming are all numbers.

Teaching Tip

Pre-partition your final number line ahead of time by making very light tick marks at $\frac{1}{4}$, $\frac{1}{3}$, $\frac{1}{2}$, $\frac{2}{3}$, and $\frac{3}{4}$. This way, as students suggest fractions you can be sure your placement of the fractions on the number line is accurate.

VIDEO CLIP 2i

Revisiting the Question, "What Are the Numbers Between 0 and 1?"

After students have completed Activity 2.2, Mr. Seay revisits the question from the beginning of the lesson, "What are the numbers between 0 and 1?" How do students' answers differ from the ones they gave at the beginning of the lesson (see Video Clip 2g)? What experiences are students drawing from to name several fractions that are between 0 and 1?

For commentary on the above, see the Appendix: Authors' Video Reflections.

7. It is likely that students will name only the fractions they have encountered during the exploration portion of the lesson. To push their thinking, you may want to ask them if there are any other numbers between 0 and 1 that could be added to the line.

8. Pose one or more of the questions in the table on page 33 to help students continue to reason about fractions as numbers.

Because the materials students used for this activity do not include rods that enable partitioning the number line into twenty-fourths, this last question may initially seem like a trick question to some students. By posing this question, you can encourage students to look deeply at the relationships between the other fractions they have been working with. The ensuing discussion can provide many opportunities for students' limited understanding to surface and for students to refine their thinking about fraction relationships.

Any of these questions can be posed during whole-class discussions, given to groups to investigate and report back, or used for assessment purposes. Allow students to discuss their thinking and provide a rationale for their responses. These questions are not designed to be answered with one-word responses and no discussion. Any one of the questions can serve as a springboard for an entire lesson.

Questions to Help Students Reason About Fractions as Numbers	
What number is halfway between 0 and 1?	Some students may initially be surprised that there are numbers between 0 and 1.
What number is halfway between 0 and $\frac{1}{2}$?	Realizing that $\frac{1}{4}$ lies between 0 and $\frac{1}{2}$ on the number line reinforces the relationship between halves and fourths.
What other numbers are the same as $\frac{1}{2}$?	Students may initially say there are several numbers here: $\frac{2}{4}$, $\frac{3}{6}$, and $\frac{6}{12}$. This is an excellent opportunity to introduce the idea that although these look like different numbers, they are actually different ways to name the same number, much like "one hundred" can also be called "ten tens." This is also an opportunity to discuss what names for the same number have in common.
What number is $\frac{1}{4}$ more than $\frac{1}{2}$? $\frac{1}{6}$ more than $\frac{1}{2}$?	This question can help students begin to reason about relative value of different fractions and compute without the need for converting to numbers with common denominators.
What number is $\frac{1}{6}$ less than 1?	This question encourages students to compare fractions to the unit.
What number is $\frac{1}{3}$ more than 1?	This question exposes students to fractions greater than 1 and can support their understanding that $\frac{4}{3}$ is the same as $1\frac{1}{3}$.
What number is halfway between $\frac{1}{12}$ and $\frac{3}{12}$?	This question provides another chance for students to encounter equivalent fractions. They can also begin to reason why there is no sixth equivalent to $\frac{1}{12}$ or $\frac{3}{12}$ (or $\frac{5}{12}$, $\frac{7}{12}$, $\frac{9}{12}$, or $\frac{11}{12}$).
Which number is closest to 0?	This provides another example of when "the larger the denominator, the smaller the fraction" is true.
Which number is closest to 1?	This can help students see that knowing both the numerator and the denominator is necessary to understanding a fraction's value. It can also provide a very reliable and frequently sufficient way to compare fractions, without needing to find common denominators and create equivalent fractions.
What would you call a number halfway between 0 and $\frac{1}{12}$?	This question asks students to extend their understanding and provides a foundation for helping them reason about fraction multiplication, such as: Why does $\frac{1}{2} \times \frac{1}{12} = \frac{1}{24}$?

2.3 Extension: Working with the Two-Unit Number Line

Overview

To provide opportunities for your students to work with fractions between 1 and 2, use the *Two-Unit Number Lines* recording sheets that are numbered from 0 to 2. (See Figure 2–8; also available as Reproducibles A and B.)

Materials
Two-Unit Number Lines **(Reproducibles A–B)**
Cuisenaire rods

1. Pass out the *Two-Unit Number Lines* (Reproducibles A and B). Have your students use the Cuisenaire rods as in Activity 2.1: *Number Line Activities with Cuisenaire Rods* to partition the number lines into halves, thirds, fourths, sixths, and twelfths.

2. Ask students questions as before, this time providing opportunities for them to reason about fractions greater than 1 as well as those less than 1.

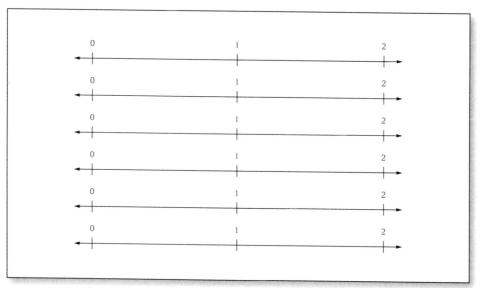

Figure 2–8. Two-Unit Number Lines (Reproducibles A and B)

ASSESSMENT OPPORTUNITY

As your students are working with the two-unit number line, don't be surprised if some of them initially identify the 6-cm dark-green rods as $\frac{1}{4}$s. This is very common! In fact, these students are correct, in that one 6-cm rod is $\frac{1}{4}$ of the distance from 0 to 2 (24 cm). What they are not considering, however, is that the unit interval is the distance between 0 and 1, and in that case each 6-cm rod is equal to $\frac{1}{2}$.

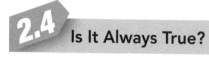

2.4 Is It Always True?

Overview

This activity will help students to examine and refine their ideas about mathematical "rules." It can also help students avoid making mistakes as they become more aware of common errors.

Materials
student-generated list of mathematical "rules" or scenarios that require students to decide on a solution

PART 1

1. Work with students to name some common rules or generalizations they may have heard about fractions. The list may include some of these ideas:

- The smaller the denominator, the larger the fraction.
- The larger the denominator, the smaller the fraction.
- You can't compare fractions with different denominators.
- Fractions are always less than 1.
- To compare two fractions, you only need to look at the numerators (or denominators).
- Finding a common denominator is the only way to compare fractions with different denominators.

2. Ask students to decide if they think the rules are always true, sometimes true, or never true. Some of the statements that students identify as sometimes true, such as "To compare two fractions, you only need to look at the numerators," can be modified slightly by changing the wording. If the statement is changed to read, "To compare two fractions *with the same denominators*, you only need to look at the numerators," it then becomes a rule that is always true.

PART 2

3. Present Scenarios A and B to your class. Ask your class to figure out what the students might have been thinking in each scenario.

By asking students to evaluate another student's faulty reasoning, we can help them to become more aware of common pitfalls and thus to avoid making those same kinds of mistakes in the future. The Math Pathways and Pitfalls program developed at WestEd by Carne Barnett-Clarke and Alma Ramirez has had a lot of success with this approach by explicitly focusing students' attention on common misconceptions. Because many of these misconceptions are based on sound mathematical ideas, the more we can help students understand the origins of common misconceptions, the more we can facilitate their development of deep and solid understandings. We can help our students become more reflective and independent learners by encouraging them to frequently ask themselves questions such as, "Does this make sense?" "Is it always true?" "What might a common mistake be?"

Scenario A: J. J.'s Solution

J. J. was solving the following problem:

Circle the larger fraction and explain your answer.

$$\frac{5}{6} \qquad \frac{7}{8}$$

J. J. circled $\frac{5}{6}$ and wrote the following explanation: *I know that $\frac{5}{6}$ is larger than $\frac{7}{8}$ because sixths are bigger than eighths. The smaller denominator means the fraction is larger.*

- What do you think of J. J.'s explanation?
- What important idea about fractions did J. J. use to solve the problem?
- Does J. J.'s reasoning make sense? Why or why not?

Scenario B: Sarah's Solution

On a different comparison task, another student, Sarah, solved the problem in this way:

Circle the larger fraction and explain your answer.

$$\frac{3}{4} \qquad \frac{5}{12}$$

Sarah circled $\frac{5}{12}$ and wrote the following explanation: *Five is more pieces than 3 pieces so $\frac{5}{12}$ is more than $\frac{3}{4}$.*

- What do you think of Sarah's explanation?
- What important idea about fractions did Sarah use to solve the problem?
- Does Sarah's reasoning make sense? Why or why not?

As we discussed at the beginning of this chapter, it is not uncommon for children to misapply generalizations as they attempt to make sense of new and complex material. As teachers, we may inadvertently contribute to this natural inclination by teaching our students to memorize so-called "rules," such as "You can't subtract a bigger number from a smaller one," "Rectangles always have two long sides and two short sides," and "The smaller the denominator, the bigger the fraction." Helping students question and refine generalizations and strategies is an extremely valuable exercise that supports their development as mathematical sense-makers. When students overgeneralize or misapply a mathematical rule, we can help them refine their thinking by asking questions like these: "Is it always true?" "Under what conditions is it not true?" and "What would you need to change to make it true?" For instance, a generalization such as "The smaller the denominator, the bigger the fraction" could be modified to read, "The smaller the denominator, the bigger the fraction *as long as the numerators are the same.*"

Making and refining mathematical generalizations is an important aspect of understanding the connections between important mathematical ideas. As teachers, we strive to help students make sense of the content we are teaching by guiding them to make those generalizations. It is often tempting to simplify mathematical principles and procedures in order to help students be successful. However, to help students build strong foundations (and to prepare them for the mathematics they will encounter in the upper grades), it is essential that we do not encourage them to apply simplified rules in a superficial manner. By engaging in the types of activities described in this chapter, you can further support the development of your students' fraction sense and help them to understand fractions as numbers in which both the numerator and denominator need to be considered in order to understand their true value.

For More Information

For more information about the Math Pathways and Pitfalls program, see www.wested.org/cs/we/view/pj/81.

Study Questions

After Reading Chapter 2

1. What information presented in the "Classroom Scenario," "What's the Math?," and "What's the Research?" sections was familiar to you or similar to your experience with students?

2. What information presented in the "Classroom Scenario," "What's the Math?," and "What's the Research?" sections was new or surprising to you?

3. Which of the "Classroom Activities" (Activity 2.1: *Number Line Activities with Cuisenaire Rods*; Activity 2.2: *Is It Always True?*; and *Questions to Help Students Reason About Fractions as Numbers*) do you plan to implement with your students?

After Trying One or More of the Activities

1. Describe the activity and any modifications you made to meet your students' needs and/or to align with your curriculum.

2. How did this activity add to your knowledge of what your students do and do not understand about fractions as numbers?

3. What are your next steps for supporting your students' learning about fractions as numbers?

Connections to *Beyond Invert & Multiply*

The foundational understandings introduced in *Beyond Pizzas & Pies, Second Edition*, are further developed in its companion resource, *Beyond Invert & Multiply*. We recommend pairing this chapter with Chapters 6, 7, and 8 in *Beyond Invert & Multiply* to further your learning.

Understanding Equivalency

How Can Double Be the Same?

Strategy #3

Provide opportunities for students to recognize equivalent fractions as different ways to name the same quantity.

CCSS Connections

Grade 3

Number and Operations—Fractions

Develop understanding of fractions as numbers.

3.NF.A.3: Explain equivalence of fractions in special cases, and compare fractions by reasoning about their size.

Grade 4

Number and Operations—Fractions

Extend understanding of fraction equivalence and ordering.

4.NF.A.1: Explain why a fraction a/b is equivalent to a fraction $(n \times a)/(n \times b)$ by using visual models, with attention to how the number and size of the parts differ even though the two fractions themselves are the same size. Use this principle to recognize and generate equivalent fractions.

4.NF.A.2: Compare two fractions with different numerators and different denominators, e.g., by creating common denominators or numerators, or by comparing to a benchmark such as $\frac{1}{2}$. Recognize that comparisons are valid only when the two fractions refer to the same whole. Record the results of comparisons with symbols $>$, $=$, or $<$, and justify the conclusions, e.g., by using a visual fraction model.

Grade 5

Number and Operations—Fractions

Use equivalent fractions as a strategy to add and subtract fractions.

5.NF.A.1: Add and subtract fractions with unlike denominators (including mixed numbers) by replacing given fractions with equivalent fractions in such a way as to produce an equivalent sum or difference of fractions with like denominators.

5.NF.A.2: Solve word problems involving addition and subtraction of fractions referring to the same whole, including cases of unlike denominators, e.g., by using visual fractions models or equations to represent the problem. Use benchmark fractions and number sense of fractions to estimate mentally and assess the reasonableness of answers.

M s. Chu's fifth graders were getting really good at finding equivalent fractions by multiplying or dividing any given fraction by $\frac{n}{n}$, such as $\frac{1}{2} \times \frac{3}{3}$ to get the equivalent fraction $\frac{3}{6}$, or $\frac{10}{15} \div \frac{5}{5}$ to get the equivalent fraction $\frac{2}{3}$. On a workbook page with several problems that asked students to multiply or divide to find an equivalent fraction, most students were able to successfully use this strategy and arrive at the correct answer. Pleased with their progress, Ms. Chu decided to provide the students with some more challenging problems on this topic to determine if they understood equivalent fractions in the context of word problems. The problems involved comparing fractions using various food items. For example, the first problem asked students to determine which child ate more pizza if one child ate $\frac{2}{8}$ of a pizza and the other ate $\frac{4}{16}$ of the same pizza.

As Ms. Chu approached Kian and Willie's table, she could tell the boys were involved in a heated discussion.

"It looks like you two are having some kind of disagreement about the first question," Ms. Chu observed. "What's causing the problem?"

"Well," explained Willie, "Kian insists that whoever eats four-sixteenths of the pizza will get more pizza than the person who eats two-eighths. I say they'll both get the same because four-sixteenths and two-eighths are equivalent fractions."

"How do you know they're equivalent fractions, Willie?" Ms. Chu asked.

"If you multiply two-eighths by two over two you'll get four-sixteenths," Willie began. "That means they're equivalent, which means they're the same thi—"

"I agree with the part about multiplying two-eighths by two over two to get four-sixteenths," interrupted Kian. "But I don't see how you can multiply something by two and have it end up being the same. Multiplication makes things bigger, and multiplying by two doubles stuff. Four is twice as big as two and sixteen is twice as big as eight. So four-sixteenths has to be bigger . . . or more . . . or something . . . ."

As Ms. Chu checked in with the other students, she found that several of them shared Kian's confusion. Many of these students had been able to use the strategy she had taught them (multiplying or dividing by $\frac{n}{n}$ to find an equivalent fraction), but when she presented them with a comparison task in context, they indicated that the new fractions were either greater or less than the original fraction.

Ms. Chu knew that she would need to help her students overcome this confusion so she asked a colleague, Ms. Dunn, how she might address it. Ms. Dunn suggested that Ms. Chu include lessons that involve fractions on a number line to help students see that equivalent fractions, such as $\frac{2}{8}$ and $\frac{4}{16}$, represent the same point on the number line and, thus, are the same number.

As Ms. Chu listened to Ms. Dunn's ideas, it occurred to her that she didn't typically think of fractions as numbers, but instead as parts of areas or sets. She knew, based on her students' class work, that they could all find equivalent fractions using the procedure she had taught them. She was also pretty confident that her students knew that equivalent meant "the same." She recognized, however, that when she provided examples of equivalent fractions on the board to help students understand the concept better, she typically drew a picture of a cake or pizza to show that no matter how you cut it up, the person who got $\frac{1}{3}$ of the cake actually got the same amount of cake as someone who got $\frac{4}{12}$:

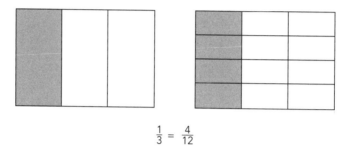

$$\frac{1}{3} = \frac{4}{12}$$

She rarely—if ever—provided an example in which she asked students to consider fractions as numbers. She began to wonder if her students had merely memorized the procedure for finding equivalent fractions without really understanding what it meant for two fractions to be the same.

E quivalent fractions are fractions that represent the same number. As described in Chapin and Johnson (2006), "[e]quivalent fractions are fractions that represent equal value; they are numerals that name the same fractional number" (114). Geometrically, equivalent fractions identify the same point on the number line. Arithmetically, when you convert equivalent fractions to their decimal form by dividing the numerator by the denominator, you end up with the same decimal.

Equivalent fractions can be found (or identified) using several different strategies. Geometrically, on the number line, equivalent fractions can be identified by adding or removing partitioning lines. In other words, in order to find an equivalent fraction for $\frac{1}{2}$, the interval from 0 to $\frac{1}{2}$ could be divided in half and the interval from $\frac{1}{2}$ to 1 could be divided in half. Thus, the interval from 0 to 1 is divided into four parts of equal length, and the number $\frac{1}{2}$ can also be called $\frac{2}{4}$ because it is located at the end of the second of those four parts:

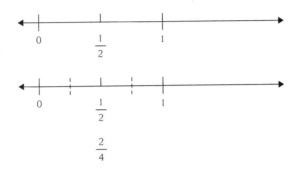

Equivalent fractions can also be found using other representations, such as area models. As shown here, $\frac{1}{2}$ can be represented as a shaded part of area in which a rectangle is divided into two parts of equal size. One of those parts is $\frac{1}{2}$ of the entire rectangle.

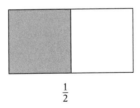

When those parts are divided in half, creating four parts of equal size, an equivalent fraction for $\frac{1}{2}$ can be seen: $\frac{2}{4}$. More important, $\frac{1}{2}$ and $\frac{2}{4}$ are the same number because they represent parts of the rectangle of equal area.

$\frac{1}{2}$ or $\frac{2}{4}$

Additional partition lines can be added to divide existing parts into smaller parts of equal size.

Arithmetically, one can find an equivalent fraction for any given fraction by multiplying (or dividing) both the numerator and the denominator by the same nonzero number, because any number multiplied (or divided) by one is the same number. (This is the Identity Property of Multiplication, which states that $N \times 1 = N$.) For instance, because $\frac{2}{2} = 1$ and $\frac{1}{2} \times \frac{2}{2} = \frac{2}{4}$, then $\frac{1}{2}$ and $\frac{2}{4}$ are both equivalent fractions and, by definition (based on the Identity Property), the same number.

D uring spring 2009, we asked 267 fourth- and sixth-grade students to respond to the following prompt:

A student does the following multiplication problem:

$$\frac{5}{6} \times \frac{2}{2} = \frac{10}{12}$$

Look at the statement below:

$\frac{10}{12}$ *is twice as large as* $\frac{5}{6}$.

Decide whether you agree or disagree with the statement.

Agree   *Disagree*

We had hoped that students would disagree with the statement. While the numerator and the denominator in $\frac{10}{12}$ are twice as large respectively as the numerator and the denominator in $\frac{5}{6}$ ($5 \times 2 = 10$ and $6 \times 2 = 12$), the value of the numbers ($\frac{5}{6}$ and $\frac{10}{12}$) is identical. In other words, $\frac{10}{12}$ is *not* twice as large as $\frac{5}{6}$. We were surprised that 60 percent of the fourth graders and 51 percent of the sixth graders circled that they agreed with the statement that $\frac{10}{12}$ is twice as large as $\frac{5}{6}$.

We also asked students to respond to a related task:

A student does the following division problem:

$$\frac{6}{10} \div \frac{2}{2} = \frac{3}{5}$$

Look at the statement below:

$\frac{3}{5}$ *is half the size of* $\frac{6}{10}$.

Decide whether you agree or disagree with the statement.

Agree   *Disagree*

Again, we hoped that students would disagree with the statement. Although the numerator and the denominator in $\frac{3}{5}$ are half the size of the numerator and the denominator in $\frac{6}{10}$ ($6 \div 2 = 3$ and $10 \div 2 = 5$), the value of the numbers ($\frac{3}{5}$ and $\frac{6}{10}$) is identical. In other words, $\frac{3}{5}$ is not half the size of $\frac{6}{10}$. Once again, we were surprised. This time 73 percent of fourth graders and 57 percent of sixth graders indicated that they agreed with the statement "$\frac{3}{5}$ is half the size of $\frac{6}{10}$."

Despite two additional years of schooling in equivalent fractions, more than half of the sixth graders in our study had limited understandings of fractions as numbers. They were quick to say that when you multiply (or divide) the numerator and the denominator by the same number, you change the value of the number.

Many students do not understand that equivalent fractions are the same number (or even that fractions are numbers). The following classroom activities will help students understand that fractions are numbers, and that equivalent fractions are merely different names for the same number.

3.1 Measuring with Cuisenaire Rods

Overview

In this activity, students use Cuisenaire rods to measure items with different lengths. By approaching the task from a measurement perspective, students begin to understand equivalencies as being different ways to name the same quantity.

1. Provide students with an item that is 12-cm long, such as a Mr. Sketch marker, and a supply of rods. Ask them, "How many brown rods long is the marker [or the item you have chosen]?" Some students will say, "One brown rod plus a purple rod"; some will say, "One and one half brown rods." After students justify their responses, remind them that the denominator of the fraction was two because the purple rod that measured the "remainder length" was $\frac{1}{2}$ of the measuring unit, the brown rod:

Materials

Measuring with Cuisenaire Rods recording sheet, 1 copy per student (see **Reproducible 3a**)

Cuisenaire rods, 1 set per pair of students

items for measuring

Manipulative Note

Cuisenaire rods are wooden or plastic blocks that range in length from 1 to 10 cm. Each rod of a given length is the same color. That is, all the 1-cm rods are white, all the 2-cm rods are red, all the 3-cm rods are light green, and so on.

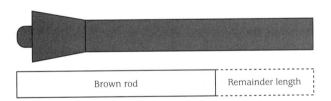

| Brown rod | Remainder length |

We call the extra the "remainder length" to provide a connection to students' experiences with division. Guide students to find that the remainder length is $\frac{1}{2}$ of the brown rod; thus, the entire length of the item is $1\frac{1}{2}$ brown rods long.

VIDEO CLIP 3a

Introducing Activity 3.1: Measuring with Cuisenaire Rods

In this clip, Ms. Thompson introduces her fourth graders to Activity 3.1. Students make an estimate of the length of a marker using brown rods as their measurement unit. What does Ms. Thompson learn about her students' understanding of fractions and measurement during this introduction?

For commentary on the above, see the Appendix: Authors' Video Reflections.

2. Have students record the length of the first item on the *Measuring with Cuisenaire Rods* recording sheet in the column labeled *First Way*. (See Figure 3–1; also available as Reproducible 3a.)

3. Call students' attention to the fact that when they used the purple rod to measure the remainder length of the item, the denominator of the fraction was two because they used the rod that was $\frac{1}{2}$ of the brown rod.

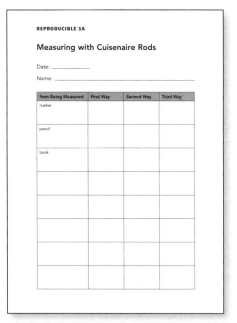

REPRODUCIBLE 3A

Measuring with Cuisenaire Rods

Date: _____

Name: _____

Item Being Measured	First Way	Second Way	Third Way
marker			
pencil			
book			

Figure 3–1. Measuring with Cuisenaire Rods (Reproducible 3a)

"How Many Brown Rods Long Is the Marker?"

Just before this clip, Edwin states that the marker was one brown and one purple rod long. Ms. Thompson agrees with Edwin and then calls Sarah up to name the purple rod in relation to the brown rod. Sarah provides the correct fraction name for the purple rod but is not able to provide a complete answer to the question, "How many brown rods long is the marker?" How does Ms. Thompson press her students to come to a complete answer to the question?

For commentary on the above, see the Appendix: Authors' Video Reflections.

Different Names for the Remainder Length

This clip opens with Ms. Thompson reminding students of their task for Activity 3.1. Then we see a group of fourth graders working on the task—specifically how to measure the "remainder length" of the marker. How can their explorations with the different rods be used to support their understanding of equivalent fractions?

For commentary on the above, see the Appendix: Authors' Video Reflections.

4. Next, instruct students to measure the marker again. They should still use one brown rod as the measurement unit, but this time they should use the red rods to measure the remainder length. After the students have found that the marker is the same length as one brown rod and two red rods, ask them to determine the correct fraction name for the red rods.

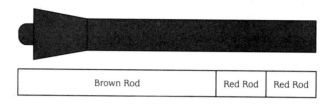

After everyone agrees that the marker is $1\frac{2}{4}$ brown rods long, point out that the denominator of the remainder length is four because the red rod is $\frac{1}{4}$ of the brown rod. Record in the column labeled *Second Way*.

Some students may initially think that the red rod is $\frac{1}{6}$ of the brown rod. This confusion usually indicates that they are comparing the red rods with the length of the marker and not with the length of the brown rod, and that they have found that six red rods are the same length as the marker:

Each red rod is $\frac{1}{6}$ of the marker but $\frac{1}{4}$ of the brown rod.

This confusion is not unusual. It provides an opportunity for teachers to acknowledge the correct reasoning that students are using while stressing the importance of understanding the measurement unit—in this case, the brown rod.

Like before, call students' attention to the fact that the denominator of the remainder length is now four, because they have used the rod that is $\frac{1}{4}$ of the brown rod.

Item Being Measured	First Way	Second Way	Third Way
marker	1 brown + 1 purple 1 1/2	1 brown + 4 whites 1 4/8	1 brown + 2 reds 1 2/4
pencil	2 browns + 1 green	2 browns + 3 whites 2 3/8	1 brown + 1 blak + 4 whites
book	3 browns	2 browns + 1 black + 1 white	2 browns + 1 green + 1 red

Item Being Measured	First Way	Second Way	Third Way
marker	1 1/2 1 brown 1 purple	1 4/8 1 purple 1 brown 2 whites	1 2/4
pencil	1 1/8 1/10 1 brown 1 white 1 orange	1 brown 5 reds 1 white	1 brown 1 blue 2 whites
book	3 5/8 3 brown 5 whites	2 brown 1 black 1 purple 2 whites	2 1/7 1/2 2/8

Figure 3–2. Measuring with Cuisenaire Rods, completed student samples.

5. Finally, direct students to measure once again, but this time have them measure the remainder length with the 1-cm white rods. Again, ask students to find the fractional value of the white rod and the length of the marker, and to justify why one white rod is $\frac{1}{8}$ of the brown rod and the marker is $1\frac{4}{8}$ brown rods long:

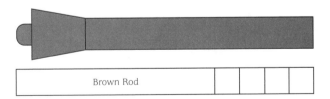

VIDEO CLIP 3d

What Do We Call Four White Rods?

Emily and her partner have found that the marker is one brown rod and four white rods long, but she is unsure of what to name the white rods. How does Ms. Thompson guide the students to help them name the white rods? How can Ms. Thompson's approach help students create a generalization about naming fractions?

For commentary on the above, see the Appendix: Authors' Video Reflections.

VIDEO CLIP 3e

Making Monica's Thinking Public

Ms. Thompson calls on Monica to show the class how she determined that the brown rod and four white rods was $1\frac{4}{8}$. How does Ms. Thompson make Monica's thinking public and accessible to the rest of the class?

For commentary on the above, see the Appendix: Authors' Video Reflections.

6. Have students measure additional items using the brown rod as the measure unit. As they measure items that are not exactly the same length as one or more brown rods, tell them to find all the different ways to name the remainder lengths. This process helps students understand why $\frac{1}{2}$, $\frac{2}{4}$, and $\frac{4}{8}$ are the same number but different names for the number or length. It also provides students with opportunities to work with equivalencies such as $\frac{1}{4} = \frac{2}{8}$ and $\frac{3}{4} = \frac{6}{8}$.

VIDEO CLIP 3f

Using the Rods to Show How $\frac{1}{2}$, $\frac{2}{4}$, and $\frac{4}{8}$ Are Equivalent

In this clip, we see Diego share something he noticed about the equivalency between one purple rod, two red rods, and four white rods, all of which equal $\frac{1}{2}$ of the brown rod. Ms. Thompson follows Diego's discovery by calling on Celeste to explain Diego's thinking. How do the materials support Diego and Celeste as they share their thinking with their classmates?

For commentary on the above, see the Appendix: Authors' Video Reflections.

3.2 Connecting Cuisenaire Measurements to the Number Line

Overview

In this activity, students build on what they have learned through the previous measurement activities to place fractions on a number line. The purpose of this activity is to help students see that equivalent fractions, such as $\frac{8}{12}$, $\frac{4}{6}$, and $\frac{2}{3}$, represent precisely the same point on the number line, and the differences in notation, or how the fractions are written, are merely a matter of which size fraction was used for the partitioning. This activity also helps students develop their understanding of numbers in terms of distance from 0, a key component of understanding the value of negative and positive integers.

Materials

Two-Unit Number Line recording sheet (**Reproducibles A and B**)

Cuisenaire rods, 1 set per pair of students, or *Centimeter-Squared Paper*, 1 copy per student (**Reproducible 3b**)

Equivalent Fractions on the Number Line recording sheet, 1 copy per student (**Reproducible 3c**)

1. Provide students with a number line that has an interval of 12 cm between the whole numbers. (See Figure 3–3; also available as Reproducibles A and B.)

Figure 3–3. Two-Unit Number Line (Reproducibles A and B)

2. Ask students to name the numbers that are halfway between 0 and 1, and halfway between 1 and 2. Have students use the rods or *Centimeter-Squared Paper* to carefully partition the number line between the whole numbers. (See Figure 3–4; also available as Reproducible 3b.) Tell them to be as accurate as possible by using the rods or squared paper as tools.

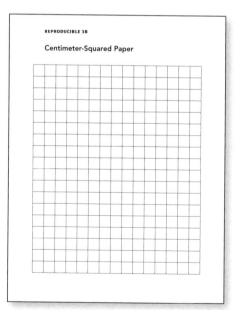

Figure 3–4. Centimeter-Squared Paper (Reproducible 3b)

3. Next, have students label these points on the number line as $\frac{1}{2}$ and $\frac{3}{2}$. Have them use the fraction notation for the whole numbers and mixed numbers as well, so that they include $\frac{0}{2}$, $\frac{1}{2}$, $\frac{2}{2}$, $1\frac{1}{2}$, and $\frac{4}{2}$ on the number line.

4. Then, have students use the rods to partition the number line further into fourths, making sure that they write $\frac{2}{4}$ and $1\frac{2}{4}$ aligned precisely with the numbers $\frac{1}{2}$ and $1\frac{1}{2}$:

5. Have students continue partitioning the number line into thirds, sixths, and twelfths, using the rods or centimeter paper to be as precise as possible. Students need to make sure that the equivalencies they are finding are carefully aligned with the previous numbers they have written. For example, $\frac{2}{6}$ should be written directly above or below $\frac{1}{3}$.

6. Finally, pass out the *Equivalent Fractions on the Number Line* recording sheet. In the second column, *Equivalent Fractions on Your Number Line*, have students record all of the equivalent fractions that are on their number lines. In the third column, Other Equivalent Fractions, have students record other fractions that are also equivalent but do not appear on their number lines. (See Figure 3–5 on page 58; also available as Reproducible 3c.)

ASSESSMENT OPPORTUNITY

Asking students to come up with other equivalent fractions can provide you with information about their understanding of equivalence. Some students may be able to generalize the pattern or algorithm for creating an unlimited number of equivalent fractions, whereas the understanding of other students may be limited to the equivalent fractions shown on their number lines.

Number	Equivalent Fractions on Your Number Line	Other Equivalent Fractions
0		
$\frac{1}{12}$		
$\frac{1}{6}$		
$\frac{1}{4}$		
$\frac{1}{3}$		
$\frac{5}{12}$		
$\frac{1}{2}$		
$\frac{7}{12}$		
$\frac{2}{3}$		
$\frac{3}{4}$		
$\frac{5}{6}$		
$\frac{11}{12}$		
1		
$1\frac{1}{12}$		
$1\frac{1}{6}$		
$1\frac{1}{4}$		
$1\frac{1}{3}$		
$1\frac{5}{12}$		
$1\frac{1}{2}$		
$1\frac{7}{12}$		
$1\frac{2}{3}$		
$1\frac{3}{4}$		
$1\frac{5}{6}$		
$1\frac{11}{12}$		
2		

Figure 3–5. Equivalent Fractions on the Number Line (Reproducible 3c)

3.3 Equivalent Expression Matchup

Overview

As students create posters that explain in multiple ways why a particular pair of fractions is equivalent, they become aware of what they do and do not understand about equivalency. This activity also gives you an opportunity to assess what your students do and don't understand about fraction equivalency.

1. Mix up the equivalent fraction cards (Reproducibles 3d–3e) and distribute them, giving one card to each student. (See Figure 3–6 on page 60.) Instruct students to find the person who has a card with an equivalent fraction. After the pairs have "found each other," have students work together to create a poster using the following criteria:

   - The two fractions must be written as an equation.

   - Include at least two other fractions that are also equivalent to your pair.

   - Provide an explanation that proves, in two different ways, that the fractions are equivalent. The explanation *may* include words, pictures, and numbers. (See Figure 3–7 on page 60.)

2. After the students' posters are completed, post them in your room and have students do a "gallery walk" to view all of the posters. Students can evaluate the posters using the criteria in Step 1 as a rubric. As students view the posters, have them reflect on which types of explanation (dividing the numerator by the denominator, showing the fractions on a number line, using area models, etc.) were most convincing to them. This reflection will provide you and your students with valuable information regarding the types of representations that best support their understanding of equivalent fractions.

Materials

chart paper for creating posters, 1 sheet per pair of students

Equivalent Fraction Cards (**Reproducibles 3d–3e**) or index cards with one fraction written on each card, 1 card per student. (To prepare your own index cards, write pairs of equivalent fractions on index cards so that only one fraction from each pair is on any one card, and each card has one or more equivalent fractions or "matches.")

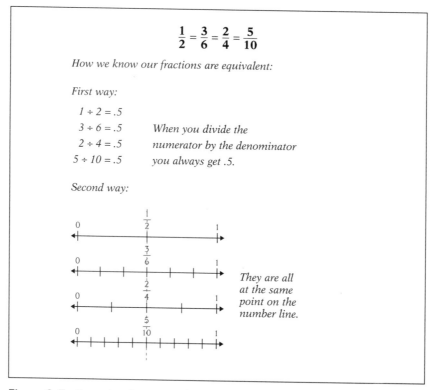

$$1\frac{5}{7} \quad \frac{7}{3} \quad \frac{3}{10} \quad \frac{9}{30} \quad \frac{4}{5}$$

$$\frac{3}{4} \quad \frac{1}{25} \quad \frac{4}{100} \quad \frac{2}{3} \quad \frac{12}{7}$$

$$\frac{3}{21} \quad 2\frac{1}{3} \quad \frac{50}{60} \quad \frac{8}{9} \quad \frac{32}{36}$$

$$\frac{1}{8} \quad \frac{2}{16} \quad \frac{16}{20} \quad \frac{6}{8} \quad 1\frac{2}{5}$$

$$\frac{5}{6} \quad \frac{6}{9} \quad \frac{1}{7} \quad \frac{7}{5} \quad \frac{8}{10}$$

$$\frac{3}{6} \quad \frac{5}{4} \quad \frac{4}{5} \quad \frac{2}{4} \quad 1\frac{1}{4}$$

Figure 3–6. Equivalent Fraction Cards (Reproducibles 3d–3e)

$$\frac{1}{2} = \frac{3}{6} = \frac{2}{4} = \frac{5}{10}$$

How we know our fractions are equivalent:

First way:

$1 \div 2 = .5$
$3 \div 6 = .5$ *When you divide the*
$2 \div 4 = .5$ *numerator by the denominator*
$5 \div 10 = .5$ *you always get .5.*

Second way:

They are all at the same point on the number line.

Figure 3–7. Example of a poster showing equivalent fractions.

To develop a deep understanding of equivalent fractions, it is necessary that students go beyond the ability to use a procedure to create equivalent fractions. They must understand that procedures, such as partitioning in the early grades and multiplying by $\frac{n}{n}$ in the upper grades, do not affect the *value* of fractions, only the way that they are *represented*. By focusing on equivalent fractions in two different ways—through measurement and with a number line—students can strengthen their understanding of fractions as numbers and the different, but equivalent, ways they may be expressed. It is well documented that a deep understanding of equivalent expressions and equalities is a necessary aspect of algebra readiness (Driscoll 1999; Falkner, Levi, and Carpenter 1999; MacGregor and Stacey 1999; National Research Council 2001).

For More Information

More information about equivalent fractions can be found in Chapter 5 of *Math Matters: Understanding the Math You Teach, Grades K–8, Second Edition,* by Suzanne H. Chapin and Art Johnson (Math Solutions, 2006).

Study Questions

After Reading Chapter 3

1. What information presented in the "Classroom Scenario," "What's the Math?," and "What's the Research?" sections was familiar to you or similar to your experience with students?

2. What information presented in the "Classroom Scenario," "What's the Math?," and "What's the Research?" sections was new or surprising to you?

3. Which of the Classroom Activities (Activity 3.1: *Measuring with Cuisenaire Rods*; Activity 3.2: *Connecting Cuisenaire Measurements to the Number Line*; Activity 3.3: *Equivalent Expression Matchup*) do you plan to implement with your students?

After Trying One or More of the Activities

1. Describe the activity and any modifications you made to meet your students' needs and/or to align with your curriculum.

2. How did this activity add to your knowledge of what your students do and do not understand about equivalent fractions?

3. What are your next steps for supporting your students' learning about equivalent fractions?

Connections to *Beyond Invert & Multiply*

The foundational understandings introduced in *Beyond Pizzas & Pies, Second Edition,* are further developed in its companion resource, *Beyond Invert & Multiply*. We recommend pairing this chapter with Chapter 3 in *Beyond Invert & Multiply* to further your learning.

Fraction Kits
Friend or Foe?

Strategy #4
Provide opportunities for students to work with changing units.

CCSS Connections

Grade 3

Number and Operations—Fractions

Develop understanding of fractions as numbers.
3.NF.A.1: Understand a fraction $1/b$ as the quantity formed by 1 part when a whole is partitioned into b equal parts; understand a fraction a/b as the quantity formed by a parts of size $1/b$.

Geometry

Reason with shapes and their attributes.
3.GA.2: Partition shapes into parts with equal areas. Express the area of each part as a unit fraction of the whole.

Grade 4

Number and Operations—Fractions

Extend understanding of fraction equivalence and ordering.
4.NF.1: Explain why a fraction a/b is equivalent to a fraction $(n \times a)/(n \times b)$ by using visual fraction models, with attention to how the number and size of the parts differ even though the two fractions themselves are the same size. Use this principle to recognize and generate equivalent fractions.

On Monday, Ms. Alvarez handed out six 15-by-2-inch strips of construction paper to each student. Each strip in the set of six was a different color. "Today we're going to make fraction kits," she told them. A few students commented that they had made kits the previous year, in third grade. "That's okay," Ms. Alvarez assured them. "You're older and know more now, so you'll be using the kits to learn fourth-grade fraction concepts."

Ms. Alvarez instructed the students to agree on the color of the strip that would be their whole. She made sure that students understood this was not the same as *hole*. After the students had chosen the strip they would use as their whole, Ms. Alvarez told them to write *1 Whole* on the front of the strip and their name on the back. She then had students choose a strip for the next part of their kit. She asked them what they thought would happen when they carefully folded this new strip right down the middle. "How many sections will you have after you fold your paper one time? What should we call these sections?" Several students responded by saying that they would have two sections and these should be called *halves*. "OK," Ms. Alvarez responded, "Write the fraction one-half on the front of each of these pieces and your name on the back. Once you've done that, carefully cut your strip on the fold so that you have two halves." After scanning the class to make sure the students were ready to move on, Ms. Alvarez told them to choose a third strip for the next part of their kits.

"I know what we're going to do next," Amy called out enthusiastically. "Fourths!"

"Let's see if Amy's prediction is correct," Ms. Alvarez responded good-naturedly. She then instructed students to fold their new strip once down the middle, and then make another fold so that they would now have four sections.

"What do you think? Was Amy right?" The students nodded their heads while Amy's tablemate, Justin, gave her a thumbs-up.

"Amy said these would be fourths. Who can tell us why they are fourths?"

Stephanie raised her hand and began talking after Ms. Alvarez nodded to signal her to begin. "They're fourths 'cause there's four of them," she said with a smile.

Ms. Alvarez told the students to carefully cut out their *fourths* and write $\frac{1}{4}$ on the front and their name on the back of each piece. She then had students choose another strip and led them through creating their eighth pieces for their fraction kits.

As she walked around the room checking on students' progress, Ms. Alvarez noticed that Taylor was labeling his pieces $\frac{1}{7}$. Ms. Alvarez knew that he had not made pieces that were the size of sevenths, but instead of correcting him immediately, she decided to find out why he had labeled his eighths as sevenths.

"I noticed that you're writing one-seventh on your red pieces," Ms. Alvarez began. "How do you know that these are sevenths?"

"Well," Taylor began. "When I counted 'em there were seven, so I knew they were sevenths."

"I see," Ms. Alvarez responded. "Is there anything else that you could do to make sure that they're sevenths?" Taylor looked up at her with a look of uncertainty on his face.

"I don't know. I thought that 'cause there's seven of them that made 'em sevenths."

"Can you tell me what they're sevenths of?" Ms. Alvarez asked in order to probe Taylor's thinking.

"I guess of the whole, but now I'm not sure." Taylor's face indicated his frustration with Ms. Alvarez's line of questioning.

Sensing that her questions were not helping Taylor's understanding of why his pieces were mislabeled, Ms. Alvarez decided that he would benefit from a more direct approach.

"When you made the fourths for your kit, what did you do?"

Taylor explained that he folded his blue strip in half and then in half again to make four equal-size pieces. He then cut out the pieces and labeled each of them $\frac{1}{4}$. As he described this process, he carefully lined up his four fourths underneath the strip that he had designated as one whole. "You see," Taylor explained. "There's four blue pieces, so they're fourths."

"I see that you have four blue pieces," Ms. Alvarez commented. "I also see that they are all the same size and when you laid out all four of them, they were the same length as your whole. So each blue piece is one-fourth of your whole. Why don't you see if the same thing will happen when you lay out your sevenths underneath your whole."

Taylor carefully laid out his seven sevenths underneath the strip he had labeled as his whole. When he got to the seventh piece and noticed that the seven pieces were not the same length as the whole, he looked up at Ms. Alvarez with a smile.

"I think I know what happened. I guess I lost one."

"What makes you think you lost one? What did you just notice?" Ms. Alvarez asked. She was happy that Taylor was aware that he was missing one of his pieces.

"Once I put all these down they should be the same length as the whole. But, I can tell that a piece is missing 'cause it would fit right there," Taylor replied, pointing to the place where the eighth eighth should go. As he spoke, Taylor began looking around and finally located the missing piece under his chair. Placing it next to the other pieces, he carefully counted and found that there were now eight red pieces.

"Now I have eight eighths," Taylor said as he began crossing out the $\frac{1}{7}$ he had originally written on each piece and replacing it with $\frac{1}{8}$.

"I noticed you're now writing one-eighth on your red pieces. Can you tell me why you're doing that?" Ms. Alvarez asked. She did not want to move on until she felt more confident in Taylor's understanding.

"Like I said, I know they're eighths because there's eight of them and that's how many it takes to be same size as the whole."

"Anything else? What about the size of the pieces?"

"Oh yeah! All the pieces are the same size," Taylor answered.

Ms. Alvarez knew that Taylor's understanding of part–whole relations was still a bit shaky, but she also needed to check in with her other students. She knew that making the fraction kit was a good start. She also knew that for Taylor, and students like him, she would need to provide many more experiences for them to truly understand what a fraction like $\frac{1}{8}$ actually means.

Representing a fractional part of an area using fraction notation involves determining the whole and considering the size of the shaded part of the area in relation to the size of the whole. In fraction kits, the whole is typically a rectangular strip of paper; however, the whole could be another shape as well. In the next figure, the long gray rectangular strip is the whole.

1 whole

$\frac{1}{2}$

Determining the size of another strip (either larger or smaller) in relation to the whole entails considering the number of copies of the strip needed to cover the whole. As shown, it takes two copies of the smaller strip to cover the whole. One of the small strips is one of two equal pieces that make up the whole. Thus, the small strip is $\frac{1}{2}$ of the whole. It is important for students to understand that the name *one-half* is not a fixed name for this strip, but rather a description of the relationship between this strip and the whole.

n 2006, I conducted an intervention study examining student learning of part–whole relations in two different conditions, both using Cuisenaire rods (McNamara 2006). For the purposes of this study, I purchased lengths of 1-cm-by-1-cm balsa wood at a hobby shop, cut them into 12-cm lengths, and painted them pink. These new rods were added to the standard set of Cuisenaire rods.

Students in one group used the Cuisenaire rods as a fraction kit, whereas students in the other group used the Cuisenaire rods as measurement tools. Students in both groups reviewed fraction notation before solving problems in which they identified fractional parts of items such as dog treats. Based on pre- and posttest results, the students in the measurement group made statistically significant higher gains during the intervention than those in the fraction kit group.

In order to explain these differences, I analyzed how the students in each group used the Cuisenaire rods. When students used the Cuisenaire rods as a fraction kit, the values of the rods remained fixed throughout the intervention. For example, the researcher-made 12-cm pink rod was always the whole; the 6-cm dark-green rod was always $\frac{1}{2}$; the 4-cm purple rod was always $\frac{1}{3}$; the 2-cm red rod was always $\frac{1}{6}$; and the 1-cm white rod was always $\frac{1}{12}$. When students were first introduced to the rods, I stressed the relationship between the smaller rods and the 12-cm rod. However, once the rods were named, students no longer had to consider this relationship to solve the problems.

Although the rods' fixed values made it quite easy for students to solve the problems, this also led many students to use the fraction names of the rods as labels and not as names (or notational forms) that reflected a relationship between the smaller rods and the whole. For example, when referring to the 2-cm red rod, students used the name *one-sixth* as though it was just the name of the rod, without needing to consider that the red rod was called *one-sixth* because of the relationship between it and the whole.

In addition, one student, Trevor, decided that the red rods were sixths not by comparing the red rods with the rod that was the whole, but merely by counting and finding out that the kit contained six red rods. When asked to explain how he had determined that the red rods were sixths, he replied, "You could just count how many it is if it's no more in the box." Trevor's understanding of why each red rod was called *one-sixths* was based on his finding that the kit contained six red rods, and not because the name *one-sixth* implied a specific part–whole relationship.

In contrast, the students who were in the measurement group solved problems in which the rod identified as the whole changed. Sometimes it might be the 12-cm pink rod; other times it might be the 8-cm brown rod. Thus, when students identified a rod as $\frac{1}{6}$, they had to consider what it was one-sixth *of*. For example, the 2-cm red rod was both one-sixth of the 12-cm pink rod and one-fourth of the 8-cm brown rod. Initially, the fact that the size of the whole changed made solving the problems more complex for students in the measurement group than for those working with the fraction kits. However, their posttest gains indicated that the measurement condition provided more support for developing their understanding of part–whole relations.

There is no doubt that making and using fraction kits can support students' understanding of foundational fraction ideas. If students are not encouraged to consider part–whole relations, however, their use of the kit may lead them to hold a superficial idea of what fraction names mean. As Deborah Ball, Dean of the School of Education at the University of Michigan, states in an article discussing the limitations of many commonly used concrete materials, "the context in which any vehicle—concrete or pictorial—is used is as important as the material itself. By context, I mean the ways in which students work with the material, toward what purposes, with what kinds of talk and interaction" (Ball 1992, 18). The following activities will engage your students with concrete materials in a meaningful way that will help them develop a deeper—and more flexible—understanding of part–whole relations and fraction notation.

4.1 Fraction Bricks

Materials

Brick by Brick recording sheet **(Reproducible 4a)**

15-by-2-inch strips of construction paper, at least 6 of different colors

legal-size envelopes for storing students' fraction kits

scissors

Overview

In this activity, students make a slight variation of a traditional fraction kit in which they refer to the whole as a *brick* and all fractional pieces in relation to the brick. This activity deepens students' understanding of fraction magnitude and fraction equivalence.

Introduce the activity by asking students where they have seen bricks used in or around buildings. Tell them that sometimes builders need to use whole bricks to cover an area like a patio or walkway, but sometimes they only need partial bricks. Explain that this activity will help them determine what to call the partial bricks.

Teaching Note

Students may want to call the half-bricks small bricks. Stress that all of the partial bricks need to be named in relation to the original, full-size brick.

1. Pass out six strips of construction paper to each student. Ask the class to choose which color to use as the brick. Tell students to write *Whole Brick* on one side of this strip and their name on the other.

> Whole Brick

2. Have students choose another strip and instruct them to carefully fold it down the middle so that they will have two equal-size parts, or sections. Ask students what they should call these partial bricks and why. Have students carefully cut this strip on the fold and label each of the resulting two pieces $\frac{1}{2}$ *Brick*.

> $\frac{1}{2}$ Brick $\frac{1}{2}$ Brick

3. Repeat Step 2, but before cutting, have students fold their strip again so they

Teaching Note

As students make the smaller, partial bricks, ask them questions such as "How many fourth-bricks are the same size as one half-brick?" and "How many half-bricks are the same as the whole brick?"

Classroom Activities

now have four equal-size sections. Have students cut and label these $\frac{1}{4}$ *Brick*.

4. Repeat Step 3, this time directing students to fold their strip one extra time. Then, ask students to cut and label these sections $\frac{1}{8}$ *Brick*.

| $\frac{1}{8}$ Brick | $\frac{1}{8}$ Brick | $\frac{1}{8}$ Brick | $\frac{1}{8}$ Brick | $\frac{1}{8}$ Brick | $\frac{1}{8}$ Brick | $\frac{1}{8}$ Brick | $\frac{1}{8}$ Brick |

5. Next, have students choose another strip and carefully fold it to make three equal sections. You will need to model this for students, as it is difficult to do it accurately. (If you prefer, have students use a ruler to measure the length of the whole strip and determine how long each section should be.) Ask students what these parts should be called. If students are unsure about what to call each of these sections, draw a table on the board to focus their attention on the relationship between the number of sections and the fraction name for each section. (See Figure 4–1.)

Bricks	Number of Equal Sections	Fraction Name of Each Section
Whole Brick	1	$\frac{1}{1}$ One Whole
$\frac{1}{2}$ Brick $\frac{1}{2}$ Brick	2	$\frac{1}{2}$ One-Half
$\frac{1}{4}$ Brick $\frac{1}{4}$ Brick $\frac{1}{4}$ Brick $\frac{1}{4}$ Brick	4	$\frac{1}{4}$ One-Fourth
$\frac{1}{8}$ Brick $\frac{1}{8}$ Brick $\frac{1}{8}$ Brick $\frac{1}{8}$ Brick $\frac{1}{8}$ Brick $\frac{1}{8}$ Brick $\frac{1}{8}$ Brick $\frac{1}{8}$ Brick	8	$\frac{1}{8}$ One-Eighth
? Brick ? Brick ? Brick	3	1/? One-

Figure 4–1. Fraction Bricks Chart

6. Finally, repeat Step 5, but before students do any cutting, have them further partition each section to make sixths. Again, ask questions to help your students understand the relationship between thirds and sixths, between sixths and halves, between all the fractions and the whole, and so forth.

7. Once students have completed making and labeling their bricks, have them investigate the relationships between the different bricks. Encourage students to refer to the partial bricks using their whole name (*half-bricks* and not just *halves*) to emphasize that they are fractions of a larger whole. Ask students to find as many different ways to arrange their bricks to cover a given area as possible. For example, when asked to cover the area of one whole brick, students may suggest two half-bricks, four fourth-bricks, one half-brick and three sixth-bricks, and so on.

8. Pass out the *Brick by Brick* recording sheet and have students record their findings. (See Figure 4–2; also available as Reproducible 4a.) Discuss and share students' solutions.

Brick by Brick

The brick company often has partial bricks left over from jobs and would like help figuring out how to use them. They know that two half-bricks will be the same size as one whole brick. In the space below, make a list of all the different ways to use the partial bricks so they don't go to waste.

1. Ways to make 1 whole brick:

   $\frac{1}{2}$ brick + $\frac{1}{2}$ brick

2. Ways to make $\frac{1}{2}$ of a brick:

3. Ways to make $\frac{1}{4}$ of a brick:

4. Ways to make $\frac{1}{3}$ of a brick:

5. Ways to make $\frac{2}{3}$ of a brick:

6. Ways to make $\frac{3}{4}$ of a brick:

7. Ways to make $\frac{5}{8}$ of a brick:

8. Ways to make $1\frac{1}{2}$ bricks:

9. Ways to make 2 bricks:

Figure 4–2. Brick by Brick (Reproducible 4a)

4.2 Pattern Block Fractions, Version 1

Overview

In this activity, students investigate the relationships between blocks when different blocks are designated as the whole. They summarize their findings in a chart that explicitly shows why a particular block, such as the green triangle, has a fractional value of $\frac{1}{6}$, $\frac{1}{3}$, and $\frac{1}{2}$.

Materials

Pattern Block Fractions recording sheet (**Reproducible 4b**)

pattern blocks, 1 tub containing only hexagons, trapezoids, blue rhombi, and triangles per 3–4 students

1. Review the names of the pattern blocks and their characteristics. It is often helpful to create a chart with this information for students to use as a reference throughout the school year.

2. Next, designate the yellow hexagon block as the whole. Ask students to find all the ways that they can cover the hexagon using only one type of block. Your students should find three ways to do this, using two trapezoids, three blue rhombi, or six triangles.

3. Ask students to find the fraction name of the trapezoid, blue rhombus, and triangle in relation to the hexagon. If students have trouble coming up with the fraction name for any of the smaller blocks, create a chart similar to the chart made in Activity 4.1: *Fraction Bricks*. (See Figure 4–3.)

4. After students have explored the relationships between the blocks and the fraction names when the hexagon is the whole, repeat the process with the rhombus designated as the whole. Students will find that the triangle, which was $\frac{1}{6}$ of the hexagon, is only $\frac{1}{2}$ of the rhombus. Be sure to ask students why the fraction name of the triangle has changed. If no one suggests that the size of the whole has changed, ask, "What did we change? Has the size of the triangle changed or has the size of the whole changed?" It is important that students realize that when the size of the whole changed, the fractional value of the triangle changed as well.

5. Before moving on, ask students what the relationship is now between the rhombus and the hexagon. Help them see that when the rhombus is considered the whole, the value of the hexagon is 3 because three of the rhombi are the same size as the hexagon. Finding the value of the trapezoid is a bit more complex. Encourage students to use what they found out about the relationship between the triangles and the rhombus to determine how many rhombi are the same size as the trapezoid. Using the triangles, students will find that one rhombus and one triangle can cover the trapezoid, and that because the triangle is $\frac{1}{2}$ of the rhombus, the trapezoid is the same as $1\frac{1}{2}$ rhombi.

Block Used as One Whole:		

Blocks	Number Needed to Cover Whole	Fraction Name of Each Block
	1	**1** **One Whole**
	2	**$\frac{1}{2}$** **One-Half**
	3	**$\frac{1}{3}$** **One-Third**
	6	**$\frac{1}{6}$** **One-Sixth**

Figure 4–3. Pattern Blocks Chart, completed

6. Repeat the process, this time designating the trapezoid as the whole. Once students have found that the triangles are $\frac{1}{3}$ of the trapezoid, encourage them to use this information to find that the rhombus is $\frac{2}{3}$ of the trapezoid, because two triangles are the same as the rhombus. Again, ask students why the fraction names, or values, of the blocks keep changing.

7. Once students have explored the relationships between all four of the blocks, have them complete the Pattern Block chart. (See Figure 4–4 on page 76; also available as Reproducible 4b.) The top row shows the blocks designated as the whole, whereas the columns show the values of the other blocks in relation to the whole.

	Whole (hexagon)	Whole (rhombus)	Whole (trapezoid)	Whole (triangle)
hexagon	1	3	2	6
trapezoid	$\frac{1}{2}$	$1\frac{1}{2}$	1	3
rhombus	$\frac{1}{3}$	1	$\frac{2}{3}$	2
triangle	$\frac{1}{6}$	$\frac{1}{2}$	$\frac{1}{3}$	1

Figure 4–4. Pattern Block Fractions (Reproducible 4b), completed

Fraction kits can be very useful tools for helping students establish a foundational understanding of important fraction concepts such as fractional notation, partitioning, equivalency, and magnitude. They can support students' reasoning about fractions and help them make sense of basic fraction computation. When used in a superficial way, however, fraction kits may lead students to develop superficial understandings of part–whole relations. Students may come to understand fraction names such as *one-fourth* to be merely the name of a piece from a fraction kit, not a name that implies a specific mathematical relationship between a part and a whole. By providing students with activities like the ones presented in this chapter, you can help them understand that fractions are always fractions of *something*, and that a fraction name such as *one-fourth* is not merely a label for a block or a colored piece of paper, but a description of a relationship between a part and a whole. In addition, activities in which the size of the whole changes, such as Activity 4.2: *Pattern Block Fractions, Version 1* can further support a deep and flexible understanding of this relationship.

Study Questions

After Reading Chapter 4

1. What information presented in the "Classroom Scenario," "What's the Math?," and "What's the Research?" sections was familiar to you or similar to your experience with students?

2. What information presented in the "Classroom Scenario," "What's the Math?," and "What's the Research?" sections was new or surprising to you?

3. Which of the Classroom Activities (Activity 4.1: *Fraction Bricks*; Activity 4.2: *Pattern Block Fractions, Version 1*) do you plan to implement with your students?

After Trying One or More of the Activities

1. Describe the activity and any modifications you made to meet your students' needs and/or to align with your curriculum.

2. How did this activity add to your knowledge of what your students do and do not understand about fraction kits?

3. What are your next steps for supporting your students' learning about fraction kits?

Connections to *Beyond Invert & Multiply*

The foundational understandings introduced in *Beyond Pizzas & Pies, Second Edition*, are further developed in its companion resource, *Beyond Invert & Multiply*. We recommend pairing this chapter with Chapters 1 and 3 in *Beyond Invert & Multiply* to further your learning.

Is $\frac{1}{2}$ Always Greater Than $\frac{1}{3}$?

The Importance of Context in Identifying the Unit

Strategy #5

Provide opportunities for students to develop their
understanding of the importance of context in fraction
comparison tasks.

CCSS Connections

Number and Operations—Fractions

Develop understanding of fractions as numbers.

3.NF.A.1: Understand a fraction $1/b$ as the quantity formed by 1 part when a whole is partitioned into b equal parts; understand a fraction a/b as the quantity formed by a parts of size $1/b$.

3.NF.A.3: Explain equivalence of fractions in special cases, and compare fractions by reasoning about their size.

3.NF.A.3.D: Compare two fractions with the same numerator or the same denominator by reasoning about their size. Recognize that comparisons are valid only when the two fractions refer to the same whole. Record the results of comparisons with the symbols $>$, $=$, or $<$, and justify the conclusions, e.g., by using a visual fraction model.

M r. Burnett's third graders had spent several days exploring basic fraction concepts. He felt confident that they really understood what it meant for something to be $\frac{1}{2}$, $\frac{1}{3}$, and $\frac{1}{4}$ of something. Mr. Burnett knew that it was important for students to encounter fractions in contexts other than just shar-

ing pizzas and pies, so he made sure to present fractions as parts of sets and points on the number line, as well. When he asked students, "Which is more? One-third of the class or one-fourth of the class?" and "Who ran farther? The student who ran halfway around the track or the student who ran one-third of the way around the track?" most students were able to answer correctly and provide a convincing rationale for their answer.

At the end of the week Mr. Burnett felt his students were ready for a task that focused on the importance of the size of the unit when making fraction comparisons. He wrote the following problem:

> Two students, Josh and Kiki, were talking about the books they were reading.
>
> Josh said he had read $\frac{1}{2}$ of the chapters in his book.
> Kiki said she had read $\frac{1}{3}$ of the chapters in her book.
>
> Which student has read more chapters? Explain your answer in the space below.

He wasn't sure that all of his students would realize that they had to know the length of the two books being compared, but he felt confident that enough students would bring this issue up so it would lead to a fruitful conversation.

After handing out the problem, Mr. Burnett was pleased to see that the students got right to work. After most students seemed to have an answer, he called the class to the rug to discuss how they went about solving the problem.

"Who would like to begin?" Mr. Burnett asked. "Remember, you need to tell us your answer and convince us that it makes sense."

Several hands went up immediately, but Mr. Burnett counted to ten before calling on anyone to allow time for more students to volunteer. When more than half the class had their hand raised, Mr. Burnett called on Emma.

"It's got to be Josh," Emma answered confidently. "One-half is always more than one-third, so Josh has read more chapters than Kiki." Mr. Burnett had expected that a few students would respond in this way, but he was pretty sure that someone would raise the question about the unknown number of chapters in the students' books.

"Does anyone have another idea? Manny?"

"I don't have another idea," Manny said. "I agree with Emma. Can I show you?" At Mr. Burnett's nod, Manny went to the whiteboard and drew two circles. "See," he said, as he drew a line down the middle of the first circle and shaded in one side. "There's half." Manny continued, dividing the other circle roughly into thirds. "Here is one-third. If I shade in one of these sections, it's gonna be smaller than the half from the other circle." Several other students nodded to indicate their agreement with Manny and Emma.

Thinking that perhaps the students assumed that Josh and Kiki were reading the same book, Mr. Burnett walked over to the class library and took two books off of the shelf. Holding up both books he asked, "Would it make a difference if Josh and Kiki were reading different books?"

At this, a handful of students looked a bit puzzled, but most shook their heads and said it wouldn't matter because $\frac{1}{2}$ is greater than $\frac{1}{3}$.

While Mr. Burnett was pleased that his students were so comfortable comparing $\frac{1}{2}$ and $\frac{1}{3}$, he was also concerned that most of them had assumed that the number of chapters, or the whole, was the same in both books. He knew he'd be spending his prep time researching and designing activities for helping his students understand the importance of context in fraction comparisons.

A fractional quantity represents a part of a whole. When comparing fractions, the size of the whole (the unit) matters. For instance, in the example described in the Classroom Scenario, there are three different possibilities depending on the number of chapters in each of the students' books. The possibilities are

1. Josh could have read more chapters than Kiki
2. Kiki could have read more chapters than Josh
3. Josh and Kiki could have read the same number of chapters

When students are working with tasks without contexts, they are expected to assume that the size of the whole is the same. However, when fractional quantities are presented in contexts, such as the one described in the Classroom Scenario, each fraction's whole may be different! Students must consider the size of the whole in order to correctly make comparisons.

What's the Research?

During spring 2009, we asked fourth and sixth graders to respond to the following:

> Patrick orders a cheese pizza at Pizza Delight. He ate $\frac{1}{2}$ of his pizza.
>
> Kevin orders a cheese pizza at Vinny's Pizza. He ate $\frac{1}{3}$ of his pizza.
>
> Who ate more pizza?
>
> A. Patrick
> B. Kevin
> C. They ate the same amount of pizza.
> D. You cannot determine who ate the most pizza.
>
> Explain your answer.

We had hoped that students would select D—you cannot determine who ate the most pizza. In this case, the pizzas cannot be assumed to be identical because they were ordered at different pizza shops and no specification is given about their size.

We were surprised to find that only 7 percent of the fourth graders and 17 percent of the sixth graders thought that it was not possible to determine who had eaten the most pizza. Those students who responded correctly offered explanations such as, "You can't determine it because you don't know if they are different sizes of pizza" or "I don't know how big the pizzas are. If they are the same, Patrick did."

On the other hand, 68 percent of the fourth graders and 74 percent of the sixth graders indicated that Patrick ate the most pizza, a finding that suggests that many students in our study compared the two fractions without considering the size of the whole. As shown in Figure 5–1, one student selected Patrick because "$\frac{1}{2}$ is bigger than $\frac{1}{3}$." Although it is true that $\frac{1}{2}$ is greater than $\frac{1}{3}$ when the wholes are the same size, this may not be the case in this problem.

> 11 Patrick orders a cheese pizza at Pizza Delight. He ate $\frac{1}{2}$ of his pizza.
>
> Kevin orders a cheese pizza at Vinny's Pizza. He ate $\frac{1}{3}$ of his pizza.
>
> Who ate more pizza?
>
> (A) Patrick   B Kevin
>
> C They ate the   D You cannot determine
>   same amount   who ate the most
>   of pizza.   pizza.
>
> Explain your answer. $\frac{1}{2}$ is bigger than $\frac{1}{3}$.

Figure 5–1. One student's written justification.

Another student drew two pizzas (circles) of equal size and shaded $\frac{1}{3}$ of one circle and $\frac{1}{2}$ of the second circle. (See Figure 5–2.) In this example, it is true that $\frac{1}{2}$ is greater than $\frac{1}{3}$, but the student did not consider whether the sizes of the wholes were identical in the question posed.

Yet another student used a common denominator strategy to compare $\frac{1}{2}$ and $\frac{1}{3}$ and concluded that Patrick ate more pizza. (See Figure 5–3.) Again, although it is true that $\frac{1}{2}$ is greater than $\frac{1}{3}$ when the wholes are the same size, the problem did not stipulate that this was the case.

Figure 5–2. One student's pictorial justification.

Figure 5–3. One student's equivalent fraction justification.

Although $\frac{1}{2}$ is always larger than $\frac{1}{3}$ when the wholes are the same, the same is not necessarily true when the wholes are different. Our research suggests that many students did not understand that, within a context, the size of the wholes must be determined before comparing fractional quantities. The following classroom activities will help students understand that, when comparing fractional quantities, the size of the whole matters. All the activities emphasize the importance of the size of the whole in relation to the part.

5.1 Pattern Block Fractions, Version 2

Overview

In this activity, students investigate the size of fractions when different pattern blocks are designated as the part. They summarize their findings in a chart that shows explicitly that a block can have several fractional names, depending on its relationship to the block that is the whole.

Materials

pattern blocks, 1 tub containing only hexagons, trapezoids, blue rhombi, and triangles per 3 or 4 students

"What Do You Call the _____?" recording sheet **(Reproducible 5a)**

1. Review the names of the pattern blocks. It is often helpful to create a chart for student reference with the names and characteristics of each block.

VIDEO CLIP 5a

Reviewing the Names of the Pattern Blocks

In this clip, we see students reviewing the names of the pattern blocks used in Activity 5.1. What teacher moves are used in this clip to ensure that all students are able to contribute to the review?

For commentary on the above, see the Appendix: Authors' Video Reflections.

---

2. Designate the triangle as *the part*. Ask students to find all the ways that they can cover each type of pattern block using only triangles. Your students should find four ways to do this because six triangles cover the hexagon, three triangles cover the trapezoid, two triangles cover the rhombus, and one triangle covers the triangle.

VIDEO CLIP 5b

Introducing Activity 5.1: Pattern Block Fractions, Version 2

In this clip, we see the introduction to Activity 5.1. Students are shown a triangle and asked to give it a fraction name. After several ideas have been presented, Ms. McNamara reminds students that to determine the fraction name of the triangle, they need to know which shape is the whole. How does this introduction prepare students for the activity?

For commentary on the above, see the Appendix: Authors' Video Reflections.

3. Instruct students to find the fraction name of the triangle in relation to each type of pattern block and record it on *"What Do You Call the _____?"* recording sheet. (See Figure 5–4 on page 88; also available as Reproducible 5a.) If students have trouble coming up with the fraction name for the triangle, you may want to refer them to the chart from Activity 4.1: *Fraction Bricks* in Chapter 4, page 71.

VIDEO CLIP 5c

What Do You Call the Triangle When the Trapezoid Is the Whole?

After naming the triangle when the hexagon is the whole, students are asked to name the triangle when the trapezoid is the whole. We see Jorge using the giant pattern blocks to justify his answer of $\frac{1}{3}$. How do the materials support the third graders' understanding of this definition of a fraction from the Common Core: "Understand a fraction 1/b as the quantity formed by 1 part when a whole is partitioned into b equal parts?"

For commentary on the above, see the Appendix: Authors' Video Reflections.

	What do you call the △	What do you call the ▱	What do you call the ⬠	What do you call the ⬡
when the ⬡ is the whole?	$\frac{1}{6}$			
when the ⬯ is the whole?	$\frac{1}{3}$			
when the ▱ is the whole?	$\frac{1}{2}$			
when the △ is the whole?	1			

Figure 5–4. "What Do You Call the _____?" (Reproducible 5a)

VIDEO CLIP 5d

Stephanie's Use of the Pattern Blocks to Support Her Reasoning

This clip takes place after students have worked at their table to complete their own charts. We see Stephanie using the giant pattern blocks to justify her answer of $\frac{1}{3}$. How do the materials support the third graders' understanding of this definition of a fraction from the Common Core: "Understand a fraction 1/b as the quantity formed by 1 part when a whole is partitioned into b equal parts?"

For commentary on the above, see the Appendix: Authors' Video Reflections.

4. Ask why the triangle is called $\frac{1}{6}$ in some situations, but $\frac{1}{3}$ or even $\frac{1}{2}$ in others. If no one suggests that the size of the whole has changed, ask, "What did we change? The size of the triangle? The size of the whole?"

5. Next, repeat the process with the rhombus designated as the part. Students will find that the rhombus is $\frac{1}{3}$ of the hexagon, because three rhombi can cover the hexagon. Comparing the rhombus with the trapezoid is more complex. Help students to see that one rhombus and one triangle can cover the trapezoid and that two triangles fit on the rhombus:

Students should then be able to reason that because two triangles fit on the rhombus, and each triangle is $\frac{1}{3}$ of the trapezoid, the rhombus is $\frac{2}{3}$ of the trapezoid.

....

VIDEO CLIP 5e

What Do You Call the Rhombus When the Trapezoid Is the Whole?

In this clip, we first see Mahalya and Haran trying to figure out what to call the rhombus when the trapezoid is the whole. Then we see this being discussed as a whole class. In the whole-class discussion, $\frac{1}{2}$ and 2 are suggested, neither of which is the correct answer. How does Ms. McNamara honor students' thinking while encouraging them to build on their understanding of unit fractions to move toward the correct answer the girls came to, $\frac{2}{3}$?

For commentary on the above, see the Appendix: Authors' Video Reflections.

....

6. Repeat the process once again, this time designating the trapezoid as the part. Students will easily find that the trapezoid is $\frac{1}{2}$ of the hexagon. However, they may need help to determine that the trapezoid is $1\frac{1}{2}$ rhombi. Encourage students to use the information they already know about the relationship between the rhombus and the triangle (the triangle is $\frac{1}{2}$ of the rhombus). This will help them see that one whole rhombus and $\frac{1}{2}$ of another can cover the trapezoid:

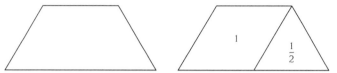

7. Last, repeat the process using the hexagon as the part. Again, ask students why the fraction names, or values, of the blocks keep changing. This question reinforces the idea that the size of the whole matters.

8. After students have had time to fill in their charts (Reproducible 5a), bring them together to discuss their strategies for naming the pattern blocks. End the lesson by asking students to reflect on the activity and respond to a question such as, "Which is larger, $\frac{1}{2}$ or $\frac{1}{3}$?" or "Is $\frac{1}{2}$ always greater than $\frac{1}{3}$?" Use the experience with the pattern blocks to reinforce the idea that fraction comparisons are only valid on the same-sized wholes.

VIDEO CLIP 5f

Is $\frac{1}{2}$ Always Greater Than $\frac{1}{3}$?

This clip takes place after students have completed Activity 5.1. Ms. McNamara asks students to respond to the statement, "$\frac{1}{2}$ is always greater than $\frac{1}{3}$." How does Matthew draw on his experience with Activity 5.1 to explain that the size of the whole matters and that, in some cases, $\frac{1}{3}$ may be bigger than $\frac{1}{2}$?

For commentary on the above, see the Appendix: Authors' Video Reflections.

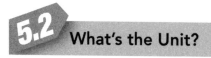

What's the Unit?

Materials

items (or pictures of items) that come in different-size packs or groups, such as

- a six-pack, twelve-pack, and case (twenty-four cans) of soda, juice, or mineral water
- batteries
- egg cartons (with plastic eggs)
- tennis balls
- sport socks

Overview

In this activity (adapted from Lamon 2005), students work with common household items to develop their understanding of the importance of the unit.

1. Hold up a six-pack of soda, juice, or mineral water (or show a picture) and ask, "How many cans do I have?" Students will respond that you have six cans. Then ask, "How many six-packs do I have?" Students will respond that you have one six-pack. Next, take out one can and ask, "What fraction of the six-pack is one can?" Students should be able to identify the can as $\frac{1}{6}$ of the six-pack. Then ask, "Is the can one or one-sixth?" (You may want to look puzzled.) Students should tell you that the can can be both. Help students to articulate that when the can is the unit, it is one whole, and when the six-pack is the unit, the can is $\frac{1}{6}$ of the six-pack.

2. Show students a twelve-pack of soda, juice, or mineral water. Ask, "What fraction of the twelve-pack is the six-pack?" Students should tell you that the six-pack is $\frac{1}{2}$ of the twelve-pack. Then ask, "What fraction of the twelve-pack is one can?" Students should tell you that one can is $\frac{1}{12}$ of the twelve-pack. If they're not sure, help them to see that the twelve-pack is made up of twelve cans, so one can is $\frac{1}{12}$ of the whole twelve-pack.

3. Next, show students a case of soda, juice, or mineral water. Ask them to identify all of the relationships between the units discussed thus far. Help students identify the following:

- One can is $\frac{1}{24}$ of the case.
- The twelve-pack is $\frac{1}{2}$ of the case.
- The six-pack is $\frac{1}{4}$ of the case.
- The case is 1 (the whole).

4. Finally, ask students to compare fractional values across the different units by asking questions like these:

- How much is one-half of the six-pack? One-third of the six-pack?
- Which is more? One-half of the six-pack or one-half of a can?
- Which is more? One-fourth of the case or one-half of the twelve-pack?
- How many cans are in one and one-half cases?

5. When your students appear comfortable thinking flexibly about the changing units in this context, have them answer similar questions about other items that come in different-size packages. Some examples include

- Batteries (may come singly, in two-packs, four-packs, six-packs, and so on)

- Eggs (may come singly, in half-dozen, dozen, or one and one-half dozen)

- Tennis balls (may come singly, in a can with three balls, in a double can with six balls)

- Sport socks (may come in single pair, two-pack, four-pack, and so on)

Helping students understand and reason about mathematical contexts is an important aspect of developing their number sense. When you engage them with tasks in which they have to consider the context and changing unit size, you can encourage them to think flexibly about fraction values. In this way, you can help them to see that when a problem is presented in a context in which the unit is unknown, the unit must be considered in order to make accurate comparisons.

For More Information

For more information about helping students to reason about changing units, see Chapter 6 in *Teaching Fractions and Ratios for Understanding: Essential Content Knowledge and Instructional Strategies for Teachers, Second Edition*, by Susan Lamon (2005).

Study Questions

After Reading Chapter 5

1. What information presented in the "Classroom Scenario," "What's the Math?," and "What's the Research?" sections was familiar to you or similar to your experience with students?

2. What information presented in the "Classroom Scenario," "What's the Math?," and "What's the Research?" sections was new or surprising to you?

3. Which of the Classroom Activities (Activity 5.1: *Pattern Block Fractions, Version 2*, Activity 5.2: *What's the Unit?*) do you plan to implement with your students?

After Trying One or More of the Activities

1. Describe the activity and any modifications you made to meet your students' needs and/or to align with your curriculum.

2. How did this activity add to your knowledge of what your students do and do not understand about the role of context when comparing fractions?

3. What are your next steps for supporting your students' learning about the role of context when comparing fractions?

Connections to *Beyond Invert & Multiply*

The foundational understandings introduced in *Beyond Pizzas & Pies, Second Edition*, are further developed in its companion resource, *Beyond Invert & Multiply*. We recommend pairing this chapter with Chapters 3, 6, and 7 in *Beyond Invert & Multiply* to further your learning.

Wrapping It Up

How Come $\frac{1}{5} \neq .15$?

Helping Students Make Sense of Fraction and Decimal Notation

Strategy #6

Provide meaningful opportunities for students to translate between fraction and decimal notation.

CCSS Connections

Grade 4

Number and Operations—Fractions

Understand decimal notation for fractions, and compare decimal fractions.

4.NF.C.6: Use decimal notation for fractions with denominators 10 or 100.

4.NF.C.7: Compare two decimals to hundredths by reasoning about their size. Recognize that comparisons are valid only when the two decimals refer to the same whole. Record the results of the comparisons with the symbols $>$, $=$, or $<$, and justify the conclusions, e.g., by using a visual model.

Grade 5

Number and Operations—Fractions

Apply and extend previous understandings of multiplication and division.

5.NF.B.3: Interpret a fraction as division of the numerator by the denominator ($a/b = a \div b$). Solve word problems involving division of whole numbers leading to answers in the form of fractions or mixed numbers, e.g., by using visual fraction models or equations to represent the problem.

M s. Alvarez's class had been working with decimal notation for fractions with denominators of 10, 100, and 1000. This year, she used the base ten materials as suggested in her teachers' guide and found that the base ten grids really helped students understand how 0.2 and 0.20 were actually the same:

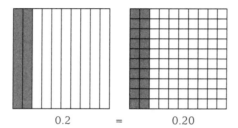

And 0.7 is more than 0.55, even though it seemed like it would be a lot less:

0.7 is more than 0.55, even though it seemed like it would be a lot less:

And 0.006 is much less than 0.6:

The grids really seemed to help students understand how to write the decimals correctly, because they could see if they were working with tenths, hundredths, or thousandths by looking at the number of sections in the grid.

When talking about decimals, Ms. Alvarez knew it was important for students to refer to the decimal numbers using the correct language, such as *three-tenths* instead of *point three*, but she also knew that the way decimals are written is often confusing for students. In order to address this confusion, Ms. Alvarez reminded the students that the decimal part of a number always begins with a *point*, and if they could remember this, they wouldn't have to worry about misplacing the decimal point. Ms. Alvarez stressed how saying the words *point one four* to themselves as they wrote a decimal such as fourteen-hundredths would help ensure they put the decimal point in the correct place.

Based on her students' success identifying decimals with the base ten materials, Ms. Alvarez felt they were ready to move on to converting fractions to decimals and decimals to fractions. She thought her students would be successful converting decimals to fractions, because the denominators were obviously 10, 100, or 1000. She was also fairly confident that most students would be able to convert fractions with denominators of 10, 100, and 1000 easily. However, she was not sure which strategies students would use with other numbers. To encourage students to use the common denominator strategy that she had introduced for creating equivalent fractions, Ms. Alvarez began by presenting students with fractions in which the denominator was a factor of 10, 100, or 1000.

She passed out a worksheet with several fractions and decimals, and encouraged students to work together to convert the numbers from one system to the other. After students had been working for a few minutes, Ms. Alvarez began to circulate and check in on their progress. As she approached Katie and Mary's table, she noticed that, in response to the decimal 0.5, Katie had written $\frac{0}{5}$.

Katie looked up and smiled at Ms. Alvarez, who said, "I see you wrote *zero-fifths* for the first problem. Can you explain how you got your answer?"

Used to Ms. Alvarez's questions, Katie began her explanation without hesitation. "Well, this is zero point five," Katie explained, pointing to the decimal, "So I thought zero would be the numerator and five would be the denominator."

Instead of addressing Katie's misunderstanding right away, Ms. Alvarez decided to check in with a few more students to see if others had made the same mistake.

When she got to Justin and Amy's table, Ms. Alvarez was pleased to see that Justin had written $\frac{1}{2}$ for 0.5. She looked at the next problem, however, and saw that in response to the fraction $\frac{2}{5}$, Justin had written 2.5.

Amy looked at Ms. Alvarez and shrugged. "I tried to tell Justin it couldn't be two point five, because two-fifths is less than one."

Relieved, Ms. Alvarez nodded to Amy. "So I put point twenty-five or twenty-five-hundredths to be the same as two-fifths," Amy continued.

"Oh dear," Ms. Alvarez thought to herself, not quite sure what to say to Amy and Justin. While she was happy that Amy was thinking about how the fractions and decimals compared with 1, she was very concerned about what their answers indicated about their understanding. As she circulated around the room, she found that Amy, Justin, and Katie were not alone in their confusion. She realized she needed some good ideas for helping students understand how the two notational systems related to one another.

A rational number is a number that can be expressed as a ratio of two integers, a and b, where b is not 0. Rational numbers are commonly represented using two different notation systems: fraction and decimal notation. Decimals that have a finite number of digits, such as 0.2, 0.002, and 0.2578, are referred to as *terminating decimals*, and all terminating decimals are rational numbers. They can also be written in fractional notation as $\frac{2}{10}$, $\frac{2}{1000}$, and $\frac{2578}{10,000}$. A repeating decimal is an expression in decimal notation that has, after some place, the same sequence of digits repeating infinitely (such as 0.333333333 . . . or 0.416666666 . . .). All repeating decimals are rational numbers and can also be expressed as $\frac{a}{b}$, in the examples shown above, as $\frac{1}{3}$ and $\frac{5}{12}$. Decimals that are both nonterminating and nonrepeating, such as π, cannot be expressed as the ratio of two integers, and thus they are not rational numbers. Rather, they are *irrational numbers*.

> ## Teaching Note
>
> The language that we use when we state fractions and decimals aloud can provide additional support for students as they think about the connections between fractions and decimals. Just as we support students in using rational number language to describe the fraction $\frac{6}{10}$ as sixth-tenths rather than six over ten, it is important to support students describing the decimal 0.6 as six-tenths rather than zero point six. By using rational number language, we can offer one additional support for students in seeing that a fraction and a decimal can represent the same number.

Converting Decimals to Fractions

Decimal notation is based upon powers of ten, and as a result, any terminating decimal notation can be written as a fraction by using the value of each place in order to rewrite each digit. For example, 0.25 can be written as $\frac{25}{100}$ because the 2 (in 0.25) represents two-tenths, and the 5 (in 0.25) represents $\frac{5}{100}$. Changing $\frac{2}{10}$ to its equivalent, $\frac{20}{100}$, and then adding it to $\frac{5}{100}$, results in the correct conversion.

Converting Fractions to Decimals

Fraction notation, on the other hand, can be converted to a decimal by interpreting the notation $\frac{a}{b}$ as a divided by b. For instance, the fraction $\frac{2}{5}$ can be interpreted as 2 divided by 5, which equals 0.4. Alternatively, for fractions that can be expressed as a terminating decimal, finding an equivalent fraction that has a power of 10 in the denominator is a means to convert from a fraction to a decimal notation. Using this approach, the fraction $\frac{2}{5}$ is equivalent to the fraction $\frac{4}{10}$, which can be rewritten as 0.4.

n 2008, one of the authors conducted a study of sixth-grade students' flexibility converting between fractions and decimals (Shaughnessy 2009). I asked 167 end-of-the-year sixth-grade students from seven different classrooms to convert fractions to decimals and decimals to fractions.

Converting Fractions to Decimals

In one task, I asked students to convert $\frac{3}{5}$ to a decimal:

Write $\frac{3}{5}$ as a decimal. _____

I anticipated that students would use one of two strategies:

1. Find an equivalent fraction for $\frac{3}{5}$ that had a power of 10 in the denominator (for example, $\frac{6}{10}$)
2. Interpret $\frac{3}{5}$ as 3 divided by 5

Suprisingly, more than 46 percent of the students were unable to correctly convert $\frac{3}{5}$ to a decimal. An analysis of patterns of errors indicated that many students were taking some or all of the digits present in the fraction notation and arranging them into a decimal notation, such as rewriting $\frac{3}{5}$ as 3.5 or .35 or .3. Although less common, a second pattern in students' errors involved dividing the denominator by the numerator: $5 \div 3 = 1.6$. Although students were more successful converting $\frac{3}{10}$, a fraction with a power of 10 in the denominator, more than 25 percent of sixth graders were still unable to convert correctly.

Converting Decimals to Fractions

Sixth-grade students also struggled to convert decimals to fractions. For one task, I asked students to convert 0.2 to a fraction:

Write 0.2 as a fraction. _____

The decimal 0.2 can be rewritten as a fraction simply by using the meaning of the place value notation: 0.2 represents two-tenths, which can be rewritten as $\frac{2}{10}$. I was surprised to find that 30 percent of sixth graders were unable to rewrite 0.2 as a fraction. An analysis of students' errors revealed two patterns. The most common pattern was that students took the digit present in the tenths place (2) and treated it as the denominator of the fraction and then placed a 1 in the numerator position—in other words, rewriting the decimal as $\frac{1}{2}$. A second pattern was that students took the digits in the decimal notation and placed them into a fractional notation—for example, $\frac{0}{2}$.

When I asked students to convert a decimal that involved an integer value, success rates dipped even further. Almost half of the sixth graders (48 percent) incorrectly converted 4.5 when shown this task:

Write 4.5 as a fraction. _____

The most common error was that students simply took the digits in the decimal and put them into a fraction notation, either $\frac{4}{5}$ or $\frac{5}{4}$. These students seem to have completely disregarded the whole number 4, indicating a limited understanding of place value, as well as decimal-to-fraction conversion.

Students' difficulties converting appear to continue well into the high school years. A recent analysis of the Long-Term Trend (LTT) data of the National Assessment of Educational Progress (NAEP) reveled not only that success converting a decimal to a fraction is poor, but that success has been decreasing over time (Kloosterman 2010). Although 61.6 percent of seventeen-year-olds surveyed were able to convert .029 to a fraction in 1982, only 29.2 percent of seventeen-year-olds were able to do so in 2004.

These findings will not be surprising to many teachers. Students' responses indicate that they understand that the two notational systems are related; however, the nature of that relationship is clearly not well understood. Students need multiple opportunities to translate between decimal and fraction notation. These opportunities need to stress the relationship between the two notational systems, and encourage students to use and develop their fraction sense.

It is not uncommon for students to have difficulty converting between fraction and decimal notation. The following activities will help your students understand that fractions and decimals are merely two different notational systems for representing the same number.

Classroom Activities

6.1 Fractions and Decimals on the Double Number Line

Overview

In this activity, students place fractions and decimals on a double number line to provide a visual representation of fraction and decimal equivalency. (See Figure 6–1; also available as Reproducible 6a.)

1. Provide each student with a double number line and post the large number line where all students can see it:

Materials

Double Number Lines (**Reproducible 6a**), 1 double number line per student

Fraction/Decimal Cards (**Reproducible 6b–6c**), 1 card per student

large double number line for modeling the activity

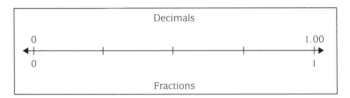

Figure 6-1. Double Number Lines (Reproducible 6a)

2. Tell students that this is a double number line and they will be writing numbers both above and below the line. Decimals go above the line and fractions go below.

3. Ask students what they notice about the number line. They should say things like, "It's from zero to one," "It has a mark in the middle," "It's divided into fourths," and so on.

> ### Teaching Note
>
> In the activities with number lines that appeared in previous chapters, it was very important for the students' partitioning of the number lines to be as accurate as possible. Accuracy is not as essential for this activity; it is more important that students are reasoning about the values in relation to one another.

4. Ask students what numbers should go in the middle of the number line. Most—possibly all—will say "one-half." Ask how one-half is written as a decimal and as a fraction and why 0.5 is the same as $\frac{1}{2}$.

5. On the large number line, model where to place $\frac{1}{2}$ and 0.5 while students record on their own number lines. Ask if there are other ways to write $\frac{1}{2}$ and 0.5 as fractions and decimals. Add a few of these (such as $\frac{5}{10}$ and 0.50) to your number line, and have students do the same:

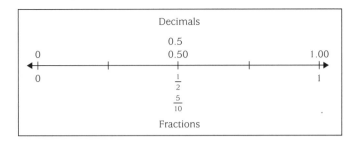

6. Next, ask what number is in the middle of 0 and $\frac{1}{2}$. Again, ask students how the number is written as both a decimal and a fraction. If students are unsure, help them to use the numbers already on the line to figure out the other numbers by asking questions such as, "What number is half of one-half?" and "What would half of fifty-hundredths be?" Record 0.25 and $\frac{1}{4}$ on the large double number line and have students record as well.

7. Repeat Step 6, this time asking what number is midway between $\frac{1}{2}$ and 1. Again, encourage students to use the numbers that they've written thus far to figure out the new numbers.

> **Teaching Note**
>
> This activity can be easily differentiated by strategically passing out the cards. For example, teachers can give more or less challenging fractions and decimals to students based on their learning needs.

8. Give each student one fraction/decimal card. (See Figure 6–2; also available as Reproducibles 6b–6c.) Instruct them to write the fraction or decimal on their number line (along with the fraction or decimal equivalent) and provide a justification for their placement. For example, a student who receives the card $\frac{1}{25}$ might say something like, "I know twenty-fifths are very tiny, so one-twenty-fifth would be very close to zero."

$\frac{1}{10}$	0.1	$\frac{3}{10}$	0.3	$\frac{4}{5}$		0.5	0.6	$\frac{3}{5}$	0.7	$\frac{7}{10}$
0.8	$\frac{1}{25}$	0.04	$\frac{3}{4}$	0.75		0.9	$\frac{9}{10}$	0.25	$\frac{1}{4}$	0.55
$\frac{2}{5}$	0.4	$\frac{1}{5}$	0.2	$\frac{1}{2}$		$\frac{11}{20}$	0.125	$\frac{1}{8}$	0.875	$\frac{7}{8}$

Figure 6-2. Fraction/Decimal Cards (Reproducibles 6b–6c)

9. Last, have students, one at a time, write their fraction or decimal on the large double number line and explain their placement to the class.

6.2 Fractions and Decimals Lineup

Overview

In this activity, students work together to create a human number line with fractions and decimals. They then complete an independent worksheet involving similar content.

1. Pass out the fraction/decimal cards, one card to each student. (Refer back to Figure 6–2; also available as Reproducibles 6b–6c.)

2. Tell the class that with the help of the cards, they will make a human number line. Indicate where 0 and 1 will be.

3. Call on students, one at a time, to place themselves along the human number line, bringing their cards with them. (You many want to call on the student who has the $\frac{1}{2}$ or 0.5 card to begin.)

4. As students place themselves along the human number line, ask the other students to provide feedback about the placements. For example, if students don't agree with someone's position, ask them to explain why and help the other student find the correct placement. Encourage students to use what they know about benchmarks such as 0, $\frac{1}{2}$, and 1. Also, ask where students should stand if they have a fraction or decimal that is equivalent to a fraction or decimal that is already in the line.

Materials

Fraction/Decimal Cards (**Reproducibles 6b–6c**), 1 card per student

Fractions and Decimals on the Number Line recording sheet (**Reproducible 6d**), 1 sheet per student

space in the classroom or in the hallway for arranging students into a human number line

---

ASSESSMENT OPPORTUNITY

Listening to students' rationales for the placement of their fractions and decimals can provide you with a great deal of information about what they do and don't understand. For example, students may think that $\frac{2}{5}$ and 0.25 are equivalent because they have the same digits. Encourage students to use what they know about benchmarks such as 0, $\frac{1}{2}$, and 1, as well as equivalent fractions, to place their numbers.

5. After the human number line has been completed and discussed, have
students complete the *Fractions and Decimals on the Number Line* recording sheet (See Figure 6–3; also available as Reproducible 6d.).

Fractions and Decimals on the Number Line

Directions: Use the number from your card to answer the following questions.

1. My number: _____ An equivalent fraction or decimal: _____

2. Place your number and its equivalent on the number line below. How did
   you know where to place your numbers?

0   1

3. From the list below, choose at least 2 fractions and 2 decimals that are
   greater than your number and place them on the number line. How did you
   know where to place your numbers?

4. From the list below, choose at least 2 fractions and 2 decimals that are less
   than your number and place them on the number line. How did you know
   where to place your numbers?

$$\frac{1}{10}, \frac{1}{8}, \frac{7}{10}, \frac{1}{5}, \frac{1}{4}, \frac{3}{10}, \frac{2}{5}, \frac{11}{20}, \frac{1}{25}, \frac{3}{5}, \frac{3}{4}, \frac{1}{2}, \frac{7}{8}, \frac{4}{5}, \frac{9}{10}$$

0.25, 0.1, 0.7, 0.125, 0.9, 0.55, 0.75, 0.5, 0.8, 0.4, 0.875, 0.2, 0.6, 0.3, 0.04

Figure 6–3. Fractions and Decimals on the Number Line (Reproducible 6d)

Overview

In this activity (adapted from Bobis 2007), students estimate the placement of fractions and decimals on an empty number line, then "flip" the number line to evaluate their estimates.

Materials

Fractions and Decimals Flip Cards (**Reproducible 6e**), 1 card per student

clothespins, 1 per student

1. Prepare the *Fractions and Decimals Flip Cards* and pass one out to each student along with a clothespin. (See Figure 6–4; also available as Reproducible 6e.)

Figure 6–4. Fractions and Decimals Flip Cards (Reproducible 6e)

2. Instruct students to fold their cards on the dotted line so that one side of the card, Side A, has an empty number line (the number line with only 0 and 1), and the other side, Side B, has the number line with the fractions and decimals.

3. Instruct students to hold their cards so the side with the empty number line (Side A) is facing them. Name a fraction or decimal and tell students to put their clothespin on the empty number line approximately where they think that number should go. For example, if you say "one-half" or "five-tenths," students should place their clothespin in the middle of the empty number line on Side A:

When students "flip" their number line so that they now see Side B, they'll be able to see how accurately they placed their clothespin:

4. Continue naming fractions and decimals for students to place on the empty number line. Students' placements should become more accurate with practice.

Overview

This activity is a variation of Activity 3: *Equivalent Expression Matchup* (page 58 in Chapter 3). As students create posters that explain in multiple ways why a particular pair of fractions and decimals are equivalent, they become aware of what they do and do not understand about equivalency. This activity also gives you an opportunity to assess what your students do and do not understand about fraction and decimal equivalency.

Materials

Fraction/Decimal Cards (**Reproducibles 6b–6c**), 1 card per student

chart paper for creating posters, 1 sheet per pair of students

1. Mix up the cards and distribute them, giving one card to each student. Instruct students to find the person who has a card that matches theirs. Once the pairs have found each other, have them work together to create a poster (see Figure 6–5) using the following criteria:

   • The fraction and decimal must be written as an equation.

   • Include at least one other fraction and one other decimal that are also equivalent to yours.

   • Provide an explanation that proves, in two different ways, that the fractions and decimals are equivalent. The explanation may include words, pictures, and numbers.

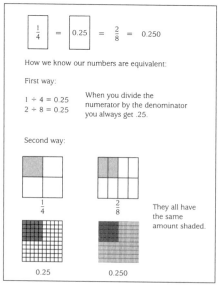

Figure 6–5. Fraction and Decimal Poster

2. After the students' posters are completed, post them in your room and have students do a gallery walk to view all the posters. Students can evaluate the posters using the criteria in the bulleted list as a rubric. As students view the posters, have them reflect on which types of explanation (dividing the numerator by the denominator, showing the fractions and decimals on a number line, using area models, and so on) were most convincing to them. This reflection will provide you and your students with valuable information regarding the types of representations that best support their understanding of fraction and decimal equivalents.

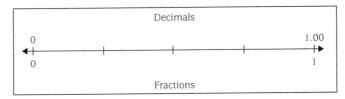

Figure 6-6. Double Number Lines (Reproducible 6a)

Helping students understand different notational forms for fractions is an important aspect of developing their fraction sense. Most important, students need to understand that fractions and decimals are merely two different ways to name the same quantity. The activities in this chapter will help your students develop a deeper and more flexible understanding of both fractions and decimals.

For More Information

- For more information about the double and the empty number line, see *Young Mathematicians at Work: Constructing Fractions, Decimals, and Percents* by Catherine Twomey Fosnot and Maarten Dolk (Heinemann, 2002).
- For more information about helping students understand the relationship between decimals and fractions, see Chapter 6 of *Math Matters: Understanding the Math You Teach, Grades K–8, Second Edition* by Suzanne H. Chapin and Art Johnson (Math Solutions, 2006).

Study Questions

After Reading Chapter 6

1. What information presented in the "Classroom Scenario," "What's the Math?," and "What's the Research?" sections was familiar to you or similar to your experience with students?

2. What information presented in the "Classroom Scenario," "What's the Math?," and "What's the Research?" sections was new or surprising to you?

3. Which of the Classroom Activities (Activity 6.1: *Fractions and Decimals on the Double Number Line*, Activity 6.2: *Fractions and Decimals Lineup*, Activity 6.3: *Fractions and Decimals Flip*, and Activity 6.4: *Fractions and Decimals Matchup*) do you plan to implement with your students?

After Trying One or More of the Activities

1. Describe the activity and any modifications you made to meet your students' needs and/or to align with your curriculum.

2. How did this activity add to your knowledge of what your students do and do not understand about the relationship between fraction and decimal notation?

3. What are your next steps for supporting your students' learning about the relationship between fraction and decimal notation?

Connections to *Beyond Invert & Multiply*

The foundational understandings introduced in *Beyond Pizzas & Pies, Second Edition*, are further developed in its companion resource, *Beyond Invert & Multiply*. We recommend pairing this chapter with Chapter 1 in *Beyond Invert & Multiply* to further your learning.

The Multiple Meanings of Fractions

Beyond Pizzas and Pies

OUTLINE

Strategy #7

Provide opportunities for students to translate between different fraction representations.

CCSS Connections

Grade 3

Number and Operations—Fractions

Develop understanding of fractions as numbers.

3.NF.A.2: Understand a fraction as a number on the number line; represent fractions on a number line diagram.

Grade 4

Number and Operations—Fractions

Build fractions from unit fractions.

4.NF.B. 3: Understand a fraction a/b with $a > 1$ as a sum of fractions $1/b$.

4.NF.B.3.A: Understand addition and subtraction of fractions as joining and separating parts referring to the same whole.

4.NF.B.3.D: Solve word problems involving addition and subtraction of fractions referring to the same whole and having like denominators.

Grade 5

Number and Operations—Fractions

Use equivalent fractions as a strategy to add and subtract fractions.

5.NF.A.2: Solve word problems involving addition and subtraction of fractions referring to the same whole, including cases of unlike denominators.

Ms. Chu was reviewing some basic fraction concepts with her fifth graders. In order to assess their understanding, she decided to have students work independently on a few problems before preparing her next lesson. The problems students worked on involved identifying fractions, making comparisons, finding equivalent fractions, and adding fractions with both common and uncommon denominators.

For the most part, Ms. Chu felt her students did fairly well on the tasks, although not as well as she would have liked. As she began planning for the next lesson, she decided to look closely at the strategies that students used to solve the problems, especially those strategies that were not particularly successful.

When she looked closely at her students' work, three things became apparent:

1. Many of her students relied heavily on drawing pictures, especially for comparison problems.
2. The drawings of more successful students varied, depending on the details of the problem.
3. Students who were less successful relied solely on drawing circles (or pizzas), regardless of the problem type or context.

For many of the comparison tasks, Ms. Chu noticed that the students who drew circles often had trouble partitioning the shapes as well as making judgments about the sizes of the parts in relation to the whole. In contrast, students who drew congruent rectangles and number lines to compare fractions tended to be much more accurate. In addition, students' use of circles extended to problems that provided a context suggesting a different representation. For example, on a problem about adding $\frac{1}{4}$ of one dozen eggs to $\frac{1}{3}$ of one dozen eggs, several students attempted to solve it by drawing two circles and shading $\frac{1}{4}$ of one and $\frac{1}{3}$ of the other. These students then had difficulty determining what to call the total value of the two quantities.

When Ms. Chu called her students to the rug to talk about their work on the fraction review, she began by commenting on all the things they had done well. She then told them she was curious about some of the strategies they had used, especially ones that didn't seem to be particularly helpful.

"There was one strategy that many of you used on the problems, and some of you even used it on almost every problem," she began. "I think I know why it's such a popular strategy, but I wanted to find out for sure from all of you."

"Maybe we used it because it's the best one!" Keisha suggested.

"Well, that's the problem. In some situations it worked just fine, but in many others, it wasn't very helpful," Ms. Chu replied. "The strategy I'm talking about involves drawing a picture. The type of picture people drew really influenced whether they were able to find the correct answer."

"I always draw pizzas," called out Ari, one of the students Ms. Chu was concerned about.

"Me too!" "Uh huh." "I like pies better!" several students responded.

"Well, that's what I'm talking about," Ms. Chu explained. "Why do you suppose pizzas and pies are so popular?"

"Fractions are almost always pizzas," Mai contributed. "That's why I mostly draw circles, although sometimes they're really hard to draw."

Mai's response gave Ms. Chu an idea. "Let's make a list to show all the ways you can think about a fraction. Let's use the fraction one-fourth as an example."

As the students called out their ideas, Ms. Chu wrote the list on the board:

- $\frac{1}{4}$ of a pizza
- $\frac{1}{4}$ of a dollar
- A quarter coin
- A quarter of an hour
- $\frac{1}{4}$ of the kids in the class
- $\frac{1}{4}$ of the population
- $\frac{1}{4}$ of a pound
- $\frac{1}{4}$ of a mile
- Quarter note
- $\frac{1}{4}$ of a candy bar
- 4th quarter
- Half of $\frac{1}{2}$

Ms. Chu told the students to look carefully at the list and talk to the other students at their tables about which items on the list would best be represented by drawing a circle and which would be easier to visualize with a different type of drawing. After sharing the ideas from their table groups, the students decided that it only made sense to use a circle to show $\frac{1}{4}$ of a pizza, the quarter (because a quarter is round), $\frac{1}{4}$ of the population (using a circle graph), and a quarter of an hour or the fourth quarter of a football game (using a clock face). For the other situations, students suggested drawing the following:

- A rectangle partitioned into four equal parts with one of them shaded (to show $\frac{1}{4}$ of a dollar, $\frac{1}{4}$ of a pound, and $\frac{1}{4}$ of a candy bar)
- A picture of twenty-eight circles with seven shaded in (to show $\frac{1}{4}$ of the class)
- A road with quarter-mile markers (to show $\frac{1}{4}$ of a mile)

- A musical measure partitioned into four sections (to show the duration of a quarter note)
- A number line (to show half of $\frac{1}{2}$)

As her students were drawing the pictures in their math journals, Ms. Chu realized that students who thought of fractions only as parts of pizza would have a very difficult time with middle school mathematics. She knew this would take some planning on her part, but she looked forward to creating opportunities to deepen her students' understanding of fractions beyond pizzas and pies.

Fractions can be represented in different ways. Three common representations for fractions that are introduced in school include the set model,
the area model, and the number line model. The fraction $\frac{3}{10}$ is represented
in these three different ways here:

Show $\frac{3}{10}$

Set Model   Area Model   Number Line Model

Understanding the relationship between representations of the same idea
is key to mathematical understanding (Cramer 2003; Hiebert 1984; Lamon
2005; Lesh, Post, and Behr 1987). Thus, translating between notations serves
an important learning function. For instance, to translate between multiple
representations of $\frac{3}{10}$, students need to construct (or reconstruct) the rational number meanings of $\frac{3}{10}$. When $\frac{3}{10}$ is translated from a set model to an area
model, students need to disregard features of the set model that are less relevant to focus on the features that are relevant. For example, the use of circles
in the set model is irrelevant; students could just as easily use boxes, stars, or
triangles to illustrate $\frac{3}{10}$. Rather, students need to focus on the total number of
the entire set of circles (or boxes, stars, or triangles) that are shaded in relation
to the total number of circles.

K athleen Cramer, Thomas Post, and Robert delMas (2002), professors at the University of Minnesota, compared the achievement of students who used commercial curricula for initial fractions learning with the achievement of students who used a curriculum designed by the researchers: the Rational Numbers Project (RNP) curriculum. The RNP curriculum emphasized the use of multiple representations for fractions, including pictorial, manipulative, verbal, real-world, and symbolic representations. In addition, the RNP curriculum emphasized having students move between different representations for rational numbers.

Fourth- and fifth-grade students exposed to the RNP curriculum significantly outperformed students exposed to standard commercial curricula for initial fractions learning. In particular, the researchers noted that students exposed to the RNP curriculum had "a stronger conceptual understanding of fractions, were better able to judge the relative sizes of two fractions, used this knowledge to estimate sums and differences, and were able to transfer their understanding of fractions to tasks that were not directly taught to them" (Cramer, Post, and delMas 2002, 128). There were no differences in students' success on equivalence items or items dealing with addition or subtraction of fractions. Given that the RNP curricula devoted significantly less time to operations, the lack of difference on addition and subtraction of fractions tasks was viewed as surprising. Furthermore, qualitative analyses of students' performance on order and estimation tasks indicated that students exposed to the RNP curricula had conceptual approaches for thinking about the tasks, whereas students exposed to standard curricula for initial fractions learning tended to rely on procedural approaches. Thus, the researchers concluded that the focus on using multiple representations for fractions learning and moving between these representations supported students in developing a foundation for more procedural work with fractions.

Helping students understand the meaning of fractions in different contexts builds their understanding of the relevant features of different fraction representations and the relationships between them. Understanding that $\frac{3}{10}$ describes the same part–whole relationship, regardless of whether it is $\frac{3}{10}$ of $\$1.00$, $\frac{3}{10}$ of a cake, $\frac{3}{10}$ of a tank of gas, or $\frac{3}{10}$ on a number line, is an important part of developing fraction sense. The following classroom activities will help your students extend their understanding of fractions beyond merely parts of pizzas and pies. In addition, the activities provide opportunities for students to reason about fraction quantities and comparisons, preparing them for operations on and with fractions.

7.1 Fractions in the Real World

Overview

In this activity, students are asked to think about where they encounter fractions outside the classroom. This helps them develop a broader understanding of fractions than relying on the concept of pieces of pizzas and pies.

Materials

a place to display the list students generate

chart paper for creating posters, 1 sheet per pair of students

1. Ask students to name all the ways they can think about a given fraction, such as $\frac{1}{4}$. List the ideas where all students can see them. Make sure the list includes examples of fractions that can be represented in the following ways:

   • As part of a set or whole number

   • As part of an area (either circular or rectangular)

   • As a number on a number line

   • As a measure

> **Teaching Note**
>
> It may not occur to some students that the quarter coin is so named because it's one-fourth of a dollar or that the quarters in a football game are each one-fourth of an hour. Highlighting these types of examples is a meaningful way to help students understand the importance, relevance, and usefulness of fractions.

> **Teaching Note**
>
> By providing the fractions for students, you ensure they are working with common fractions for which there should be many examples.

2. Ask students to suggest what kind of drawing they would make to represent each example from the list. Sketch a few of the students' suggestions or have students come up and sketch them. As the examples are sketched, identify the different types of representations for students.

3. Write the following fractions where all students can see them: $\frac{1}{10}, \frac{1}{8}, \frac{1}{5}, \frac{1}{3}, \frac{1}{2}, \frac{3}{5}, \frac{2}{3}, \frac{3}{4}$, and $\frac{7}{8}$. Tell each student pair to choose a fraction from the list and write down at least one example of each type of representation for their fraction. For example, a pair of students who pick $\frac{1}{10}$ might write:

   • One cake shared among ten people (area model using a rectangle)

   • A pizza divided into ten equal pieces (area model using a circle)

- One piece of gum from a package of gum that has ten pieces in it (set model)

- A segment marked *0* to *1* on a number line where the segment is divided into ten equal sections (number line)

- A track showing one-tenth mile markers (measure)

4. After students have created their lists, have them make a poster with words, numbers, and pictures showing all the different examples of their fraction. (See Figure 7–1.)

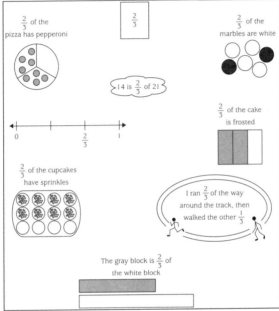

Figure 7–1. Fractions Examples Poster

7.2 Exploring Fraction Representations

Overview

In this activity, students use the posters made in Activity 7.1: *Fractions in the Real World* to generate a list of the types of fraction problems that use a particular representation.

Materials

posters from Activity 7.1: *Fractions in the Real World*

large sheets of construction or chart paper, 1 sheet per group of 4–6 students

1. Focus students' attention on the posters from Activity 7.1: *Fractions in the Real World*. Lead a discussion about the different ways the fractions on each poster are represented. Be sure to point out that fractions can be shown as part of a set or part of a whole number, as part of an area (either circular or rectangular), as a number on a number line, or as a measure.

2. Arrange students in small groups of four to six. Assign each group a type of fraction representation (part of a set or whole number, part of a circle, part of a rectangle, a number on a number line, or a measure) to investigate and report on. Instruct students to look at all the posters and make a list describing all the contexts in which their assigned representation is shown on the different posters.

3. Last, have each group write a comparison and an addition or a subtraction problem that can be solved using their assigned representation. (See Figure 7–2.)

4. Have groups write their problems on large paper and post them for other students to solve.

Representation	Sample Comparison Task	Sample Addition/Subtraction Task
Set or Whole Number	In Mr. A's class there are 24 students. One-third of the students play soccer. In Ms. B's class there are 20 students. One-half of the students play soccer. Which class has more soccer players?	Mr. A's class has 24 students and only 2 choices of musical instrument. One-third of the students play the violin and $\frac{1}{6}$ of the students play cello. How many students in Mr. A's class play an instrument?
Area of a Circle	Jasmine and Brendan were comparing how long they worked on their homework. Jasmine worked for $\frac{7}{12}$ of an hour; Brendan worked for $\frac{3}{4}$ of an hour. Who spent more time on their homework?	In the morning I watched TV for $\frac{1}{3}$ of an hour. In the afternoon I watched TV for $\frac{1}{2}$ an hour. How long did I watch TV?
Area of a Rectangle	My twin brother and I love brownies! Our dad made us each our own pan of brownies for our birthday. (We have two pans that are exactly the same size.) I ate $\frac{5}{8}$ of my pan; my brother ate $\frac{2}{3}$ of his pan. Which one of us ate more?	My sister offered to share a candy bar with me. She ate $\frac{3}{8}$ of it. How much of the candy bar did I get?
Number Line	Which number is greater, $\frac{7}{8}$ or $\frac{4}{5}$?	What is $\frac{1}{4} + \frac{1}{2}$?
Measure	My friend and I wanted to see who could run the farthest without stopping, so we tried to run from our school to our favorite yogurt shop. I ran $\frac{13}{16}$ of the way; my friend ran $\frac{9}{10}$ of the way. Which one of us ran farther?	I walked $\frac{4}{9}$ of the way home from school with my friend. Then I walked part of the way by myself. I ran into my mom and walked the final $\frac{2}{9}$ of the way with her. How much of the way home did I walk by myself?

Figure 7–2. Fraction Representations

7.3 Extension: Fraction Representation Problems

Overview

In this activity, students work in pairs to write fraction problems that can be solved using a given representation. Students then trade with other pairs and solve the problems they have written.

Materials

posters from Activity 7.1: *Fractions in the Real World*

Fraction Representation Cards (**Reproducible 7a**), 1 set of cards per pair of students

individual whiteboards or notebook paper, 1 set of cards per pair of students

1. Refer students to the posters from Activity 7.1: *Fractions in the Real World*.

2. Pass out the *Fraction Representation Cards* and whiteboards or notebook paper to student pairs. (See Figure 7–3; also available as Reproducible 7a.)

3. Tell students that their task is to write a fraction problem that can be solved using the representation on their card. For example, if their card says "area model: rectangle," they need to write a problem that can be solved using one or more rectangles. (Refer back to Figure 7–2 for examples of problem types.)

4. Have students show you their problems and check them for appropriate use of the representation. After students have a correctly written problem, they can trade with other students whose problems have also been approved and solve them in their math journals or on separate pieces of paper.

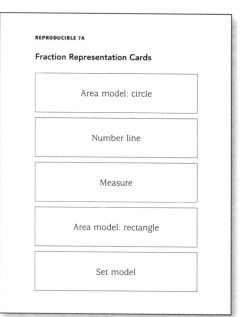

Figure 7–3. Fraction Representation Cards (Reproducible 7a)

Fraction sense involves having a flexible and broad understanding of fraction uses and representations. By seeing a given fraction expressed using a variety of representations, students can begin to recognize the commonality between different ways of representing the same fraction. Helping students know what representations make sense in different contexts can support their ability to reason about fractions and solve many different types of problems involving fractions. This understanding is essential as students begin to perform computations on and with fractions.

Study Questions

After Reading Chapter 7

1. What information presented in the "Classroom Scenario," "What's the Math?," and "What's the Research?" sections was familiar to you or similar to your experience with students?

2. What information presented in the "Classroom Scenario," "What's the Math?," and "What's the Research?" sections was new or surprising to you?

3. Which of the Classroom Activities (Activity 7.1: *Fractions in the Real World*, Activity 7.2: *Exploring Fraction Representation*, Activity 7.2 Extension: *Fraction Representation Problems*) do you plan to implement with your students?

After Trying One or More of the Activities

1. Describe the activity and any modifications you made to meet the needs of your students and/or to align with your curriculum.

2. How did this activity add to your knowledge of what your students do and do not understand about the multiple meanings of fractions?

3. What are your next steps for supporting your students' learning about the multiple meanings of fractions?

Connections to *Beyond Invert & Multiply*

The foundational understandings introduced in *Beyond Pizzas & Pies, Second Edition*, are further developed in its companion resource, *Beyond Invert & Multiply*. We recommend pairing this chapter with Chapters 3 and 4 in *Beyond Invert & Multiply* to further your learning.

Comparing Fractions
Do You Always Need a Common Denominator?

8

Strategy #8

Provide students with multiple strategies for comparing and reasoning about fractions.

CCSS Connections

Grade 3

Number and Operations—Fractions

Develop understanding of fractions as numbers.

3.NF.A.3: Explain equivalence of fractions in special cases, and compare fractions by reasoning about their size.

Grade 4

Number and Operations—Fractions

Extend understanding of fraction equivalence and ordering.

4.NF.A.1: Explain why a fraction a/b is equivalent to a fraction $(n \times a)/(n \times b)$ by using visual fraction models, with attention to how the number and size of the parts differ even though the two fractions themselves are the same size. Use this principle to recognize and generate equivalent fractions.

4.NF.A.2: Compare two fractions with different numerators and different denominators, e.g., by creating common denominators or numerators, or by comparing to a benchmark such as $\frac{1}{2}$. Recognize that comparisons are valid only when the two fractions refer to the same whole. Record the results of comparisons with symbols $>$, $=$, or $<$, and justify the conclusions, e.g., by using a visual fraction model.

M s. Alvarez's fourth graders had been studying fractions for several weeks when they encountered the following problem in their textbook:

Use a common denominator to compare these fractions. Write >, <, or = in the box.

1. $\frac{2}{7} \ \Box \ \frac{3}{5}$ 5. $\frac{1}{2} \ \Box \ \frac{3}{4}$

2. $\frac{8}{9} \ \Box \ \frac{1}{3}$ 6. $\frac{5}{6} \ \Box \ \frac{5}{8}$

3. $\frac{1}{2} \ \Box \ \frac{4}{8}$ 7. $\frac{6}{7} \ \Box \ \frac{7}{6}$

4. $\frac{3}{4} \ \Box \ \frac{5}{6}$ 8. $\frac{7}{12} \ \Box \ \frac{9}{20}$

After the students worked for a while, Ms. Alvarez noticed that several of them looked quite annoyed. She decided to find out what was causing the problem. She approached Amy and Justin's table. When she looked down at their papers she saw they had answered all the problems correctly.

"You two look upset. What seems to be the problem?" asked Ms. Alvarez.

"Ms. A," whined Justin, "We can't do this. We know how to compare all the fractions, but neither of us has any idea why we need to find a common denominator. Are we going to get marked down if we don't?"

"I don't even remember what a common denominator is!" Amy piped in.

"Hmm . . . Why don't you tell me how you compared two-sevenths and three-fifths? Then we'll see if you need a common denominator to compare these fractions."

"For this one," Justin began, pointing to the first problem, "I knew that two-sevenths is less than a half, and three-fifths is more than a half, so two-sevenths has to be less than three-fifths."

"How did you know that two-sevenths is less than one-half?" asked Ms. Alvarez.

"Well, because if you have sevenths, you'd have to have three and a half of them to be exactly one-half, and two-sevenths is less than that. It's the same thing with the fifths. Two and a half-fifths would be exactly a half, so three-fifths is more than half."

"OK, that makes sense to me," Ms. Alvarez responded. She was pleased with their strategy of using one-half as a benchmark fraction. "How did you compare the next one: eight-ninths and one-third?"

"Well, that one is kind of the same, except we thought about if the fractions were closer to one or zero instead of one-half," Amy began. "Eight-ninths is really close to one because ninths are small, so eight of them would be almost the whole thing, and one-third is only third of the way from zero to one. Even if you had two-thirds it would still be less than eight-ninths!"

"Interesting ideas," Ms. Alvarez commented. She jotted herself a note on her clipboard. "I'm going to check in with the other students. Would you two be prepared to share your thinking about numbers one and two when we discuss these as a class?" Amy and Justin nodded.

Ms. Alvarez moved on to Dante and Haley's table to find out how they compared one-half and four-eighths.

"Easy!" the students said at the same time. Haley continued, "One is half of two, and four is half of eight, so those two have to be equal."

Ms. Alvarez quickly wrote a note on her ever-present clipboard. "Will you share your idea in a few minutes?"

"OK."

Seeing Salim's hand in the air, Ms. Alvarez went to his table next.

"I want to discuss this one: three-fourths and five-sixths," Salim said. "I wasn't sure about it at first. I thought they might be equal since three is just one less than four, and five is just one less than six, but then Enrique helped me see that since fourths are bigger than sixths, more is missing in the three-fourths than in the five-sixths. So five-sixths is closer to the whole thing than three-fourths. I was trying to solve it with pizzas, but Enrique showed it to me on a number line and it made more sense."

"Thanks for helping Salim, Enrique. You two are a good team," Ms. Alvarez remarked. The boys smiled. "Will you two report on this problem in Whole Group? It would be especially helpful for the rest of the class to hear how you worked as a team to solve it." The smiles grew wider.

Ms. Alvarez continued, "I'm curious about how you solved the next problem, comparing one-half and three-fourths."

"Well, everybody knows that two-fourths is the same as one-half, so three-fourths has to be bigger than one-half," Enrique declared with authority.

Moving on, Ms. Alvarez stopped at Kelsey and Matthew's table next. "What did you two think about number six, comparing five-sixths and five-eighths?"

"That one was super easy," Matthew exclaimed. "Sixths are bigger than eighths—remember how you showed us that when we were talking about sharing our favorite pizza? We would much rather share with six people, 'cause we know we'll get a bigger piece! So if you have the same number of sixths and eighths, five of those sixths is for sure gonna be more than five of those little eighths."

"I'm glad thinking about the pizzas helped you with this problem. Will you share that with the class during Whole Group?" Matthew and Kelsey nodded as Ms. Alvarez moved on to the next group.

"Ms. A, they were trying to confuse us with number seven," Lila exclaimed.

"Yeah, for sixth-sevenths and seven-sixths, they used the same numbers but switched them around," her partner, Dana, added. "But all we had to think about was, 'What makes a whole?' Since seven-sevenths is the same as one, six-sevenths is one-seventh less than one, or less than the whole. Seven-sixths is more than one, 'cause six-sixths equals one. So, six-sevenths is less than seven-sixths," Dana looked satisfied, happy that she and Lila hadn't been "fooled." "Can we share this one during Whole Group?"

"That would be great," Ms. Alvarez responded, pleased that Lila and Dana were so enthusiastic about sharing their ideas with the class.

Before bringing the class together for a whole-group discussion of the problems, Ms. Alvarez stopped at Tiffany and Solomon's table to find out how they compared $\frac{7}{12}$ and $\frac{9}{20}$. "How did you two do with number eight?" she asked.

"It had me a little stumped at first," Tiffany began. "I mean, I was pretty certain that seven-twelfths is more than nine-twentieths, but not really sure how to explain it. Then Solomon started acting very silly, waving his hands in front of my face and saying, 'Think about one-half, think about one-half,' in a weird and spooky voice. I thought he'd finally gone crazy but then I realized that seven-twelfths and nine-twentieths are both close to one-half, only seven-twelfths is one-twelfth more than a half, and nine-twentieths is one-twentieth less than one-half. I was glad Solomon hadn't gone crazy and also happy that he helped me figure it out."

"I'm glad, too," Ms. Alvarez said with a smile. "When we go over these problems in Whole Group, will you be sure to share this strategy with the rest of the class?"

Ms. Alvarez headed back to the front of the room to call for attention and begin a whole-group discussion of students' comparison strategies. She was pleased with how her students had worked together to solve the problems. She was also pleased to see how much number sense they seemed to have. She knew she would have to review how to find and use common denominators, but she also realized that she would need to do it in a way that respected and built on her students' fraction sense. To do it in any other way would be a disservice to her students.

When comparing fractions, students need to consider the size of the wholes *and* interpret each fraction as a single number defined by the relationship between the numerator and the denominator.

Fractions can be compared in several different ways—finding a common denominator or cross-multiplying to compare are two common approaches that students learn in school. However, these approaches do not require a consideration of the size of the fractions. Alternative comparison strategies may also support reasoning about the size of the fractions. These strategies include.

- same number of parts but parts of different sizes (same numerators);
- more and less than one-half or one whole; and
- closeness to one-half or one whole (Van de Walle, Karp, and Bay-Williams 2009).

Although finding a common denominator, finding a common numerator, and cross-multiplying are useful comparison strategies in all cases, the "more and less than one-half or one whole" and the "closeness to one-half or one whole" strategies work only in particular cases. (See Figure 8–1.)

Strategy	Example
Common denominator	$\frac{1}{4}$ and $\frac{2}{3}$ $\frac{1}{4} \times \frac{3}{3} = \frac{3}{12}$ $\frac{2}{3} \times \frac{4}{4} = \frac{8}{12}$ $\frac{3}{12} < \frac{8}{12}$
Cross-multiplying	$\frac{1}{4}$ ☐ $\frac{2}{3}$ 1×3 ☐ 4×2 3 ☐ 8 $3 < 8$ So, $\frac{1}{4} < \frac{2}{3}$.
Same number of parts but parts of different sizes (same numerators)	$\frac{1}{4}$ and $\frac{2}{3}$ $\frac{1}{4} \times \frac{2}{2} = \frac{2}{8}$ $\frac{2}{8}$ and $\frac{2}{3}$ Eighths are smaller than thirds. $\frac{2}{8} < \frac{2}{3}$ So, $\frac{1}{4} < \frac{2}{3}$.
More and less than one-half or one whole	$\frac{1}{4}$ and $\frac{2}{3}$ $\frac{1}{4}$ is less than $\frac{1}{2}$; $\frac{2}{3}$ is more than $\frac{1}{2}$ $\frac{1}{4} < \frac{2}{3}$
Closeness to one-half or one whole	$\frac{3}{4}$ and $\frac{4}{5}$ $\frac{3}{4}$ is $\frac{1}{4}$ away from 1 whole; $\frac{4}{5}$ is $\frac{1}{5}$ away from 1 whole. $\frac{1}{4}$ is greater than $\frac{1}{5}$ because fourths are larger than fifths. $\frac{4}{5}$ is closer to 1. $\frac{3}{4} < \frac{4}{5}$

Figure 8–1. Strategies for Comparing Fractions

Helping students develop their "fraction sense" is extremely important before they begin computing on and with fractions. We've all seen students who are able to arrive at a correct answer to a problem such as $\frac{1}{4} + \frac{1}{8} = \frac{3}{8}$, but have no way of determining whether their answer makes sense. By comparing fractions with benchmarks such as zero, one-half, and one, students can reason about fraction values, often solving comparison and ordering problems quickly and without the need for paper and pencil. Students without this type of understanding are seriously limited in their abilities to reason about, and make sense of, fractions.

A frequently reported finding from the 1996 NAEP test (National Assessment of Educational Progress) involves the response of thirteen-year-olds to the following item:

Estimate the answer to $\frac{12}{13} + \frac{7}{8}$. You will not have time to solve the problem using pencil and paper.

Answer choices were *1, 2, 19, 21,* and *I don't know.*

Only 24 percent of the students tested chose the correct answer, 7 percent chose *1,* 28 percent chose *19,* 27 percent chose *21,* and 14 percent chose *I don't know.* These findings indicate that very few of the students (less than 25 percent!) were able to look at $\frac{12}{13}$ and $\frac{7}{8}$ and think, "Those are both close to one, so the only answer that makes sense is two."

Professors and researchers from University of Missouri-Columbia Barbara Reys, Ok-Kyeong Kim, and Jennifer Bay (1999) investigated fifth-grade students' use of benchmarks to think about and solve problems involving fractions by interviewing them after the students had had instruction on comparing, ordering, adding, and subtracting fractions. Reys, Kim, and Bay asked twenty students to respond to the following three prompts:

1. Think about the fraction $\frac{2}{5}$. What can you tell me about it? Prepare a "report" for me about the fraction $\frac{2}{5}$.

2. At a party, several large pizzas were ordered. Jake, John, and Josh each ate a different kind of pizza. Jake ate $\frac{1}{3}$ of a pepperoni pizza, John ate $\frac{4}{8}$ of a veggie pizza, and Josh ate $\frac{3}{5}$ of a cheese pizza. Who ate the most pizza? Explain how you know.

3. Are the following sums larger or smaller than 1? Explain how you know. (Encourage students to use estimation.)

   a. $\frac{3}{8} + \frac{4}{9}$
   b. $\frac{1}{2} + \frac{1}{3}$

The researchers found that students rarely used one-half as a benchmark for solving the problems. Also, in response to the first prompt, "Think about the fraction two-fifths. What can you tell me about it?" more than one-third of the students interviewed drew figures that showed no attempt to create equal-size parts for the fifths.

For the second prompt, in which students were asked to compare $\frac{1}{3}$, $\frac{4}{8}$, and $\frac{3}{5}$, 25 percent of the students used common denominators to convert the fractions before comparing them. This computation was unnecessary, however, because all three fractions could easily be compared with $\frac{1}{2}$. When asked why they used the common denominator strategy, several students indicated that using that strategy was "doing math."

The students' responses to Question 3a, involving estimation—Is $\frac{3}{8} + \frac{4}{9}$ larger or smaller than 1?—again demonstrated limited knowledge of how to use one-half as a benchmark to reason about the answer to $\frac{3}{8} + \frac{4}{9}$. Only three of twenty students gave an estimate of "about 1"; the remaining seventeen students were unable to reason about the solution without being allowed to find the exact answer. Students were far more successful with the final item—Is $\frac{1}{2} + \frac{1}{3}$ larger or smaller than 1?—but even so, just over half of them (60 percent, or twelve of twenty) were able to provide a reasonable answer. The remaining eight students either applied incorrect algorithms, guessed, or gave up.

These findings indicate that limiting students' strategies for comparing and ordering fractions to using a common denominator is unlikely to help students develop an understanding of fraction values. In the classroom scenario presented at the beginning of the chapter, Ms. Alvarez's students were annoyed about the need to find a common denominator because they had very successful strategies for approaching the comparison tasks using their knowledge of benchmark fractions and the magnitude of unit fractions (fractions with a denominator of 1). When students use a procedure for finding a common denominator, they often lose track of the meaning of the numbers and provide nonsensical answers.

There will certainly be instances when the only, or most efficient, means of comparing fractions involves the use of a common denominator. However, whenever possible, teachers should encourage learners to use strategies like the ones used by Ms. Alvarez's students that support the development of learners' fraction sense. The following classroom activities will help students understand how to use benchmarks such as 0, $\frac{1}{2}$, and 1 to compare fractions as an alternative to finding a common denominator. They stress reasoning rather than computation.

8.1 More or Less Than $\frac{1}{2}$?

Overview

In this activity, students explore the relationship between numerators and denominators to help them reason about fraction magnitude in relation to the benchmark $\frac{1}{2}$.

1. After students have made a Fraction Kit (see Chapter 4 for directions for making Fraction Kits), have them cut the *Right Half of Number Line* sheet where indicated and tape it to the *Left Half of Number Line* sheet to make several stacked number lines, each fifteen inches long. (The number line templates are available as Reproducibles 8a and 8b.)

Materials
complete set of Stacked Number Lines *(Left Half of Number Line* and *Right Half of Number Line* recording sheets), per student (**Reproducibles 8a–8b**)
Fraction Kits with halves, thirds, fourths, sixths, and eighths

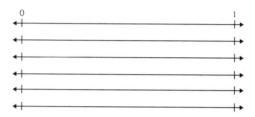

Have students check to make sure that the unit distance (the distance from 0 to 1) is the same as the length of the whole from the Fraction Kit.

VIDEO CLIP 8a

Introducing Activity 8.1: More or Less Than $\frac{1}{2}$?

In this clip, we see Ms. Kretschmar introducing her students to Activity 8.1. She makes a point of asking students to make sure she "did her homework," and made number lines with a unit distance that is the same length as the "whole" piece from the fraction kits they made during a previous lesson. Why is it important that students make this comparison?

For commentary on the above, see the Appendix: Authors' Video Reflections.

2. Have students use the $\frac{1}{2}$ pieces from their Fraction Kit to partition the second number line to show $\frac{0}{2}$, $\frac{1}{2}$, and $\frac{2}{2}$.

VIDEO CLIP 8b

Labeling the Number Line

In this clip, we see Ms. Kretschmar modeling for students how to partition and label the number line using the $\frac{1}{2}$ pieces from their fraction kits. Ms. Kretschmar is very explicit about where to place the numbers $\frac{1}{2}$ and $\frac{2}{2}$ on the number line. Why might labeling the number line be challenging for students as they transition from working with the fraction kit to the number line?

For commentary on the above, see the Appendix: Authors' Video Reflections.

3. Next, have students use the $\frac{1}{3}$ pieces from their Fraction Kits to partition the third number line to show $\frac{0}{3}$, $\frac{1}{3}$, $\frac{2}{3}$, and $\frac{3}{3}$.

4. Have students proceed in this manner until all the remaining number lines have been partitioned.

5. When all the number lines have been partitioned, ask students to identify all the fractions that they labeled that are equivalent to $\frac{1}{2}$ and write them in a chart like the one shown here:

$<\frac{1}{2}$	$=\frac{1}{2}$	$>\frac{1}{2}$
	$\frac{2}{4}$	
	$\frac{3}{6}$	
	$\frac{4}{8}$	

6. Lead a class discussion on what students notice about the relationship between the numerators and denominators of all these fractions. If students don't mention that the numerator is always half of the denominator, ask guiding questions, such as, "Look at the fraction two-fourths. What is the denominator? What number is half of the denominator?" to help them come to this realization.

VIDEO CLIP 8c

Fractions That Equal $\frac{1}{2}$

In this clip, students have already used their fraction kits to partition their number lines. We now see several students share their ideas about fractions that are equal to $\frac{1}{2}$. How does students' work with the fraction kits and number lines help them identify, reason about, and communicate about fractions equal to $\frac{1}{2}$?

For commentary on the above, see the Appendix: Authors' Video Reflections.

VIDEO CLIP 8d

Describing the Relationship Between the Numerator and Denominator in Fractions Equal To $\frac{1}{2}$

In this clip, Ms. Kretschmar revisits an observation made by Leo and RaSean that, in fractions equal to one-half, the "numinator [sic] is gonna be half of that number [the denominator]." Ms. Kretschmar calls on several students to repeat this idea and charts students' responses. How does the teacher's move of asking students to repeat Leo and RaSean's observation create opportunities for more students to understand this important idea?

For commentary on the above, see the Appendix: Authors' Video Reflections.

7. Next, have students identify all the fractions that they labeled that are less than $\frac{1}{2}$, and repeat the discussion about the relationship between the numerators and denominators. Students should notice that all the numerators are less than half of the denominators (e.g., 1 is less than half of 4, so $\frac{1}{4}$ is less than $\frac{1}{2}$, and 3 is less than half of 8, so $\frac{3}{8}$ is less than $\frac{1}{2}$).

VIDEO CLIP 8e

Reasoning About Fractions Less Than $\frac{1}{2}$

After discussing the characteristics of fractions that equal $\frac{1}{2}$, students identify fractions on their number lines that are less than $\frac{1}{2}$. How does students' work with the fraction kits and number lines help them identify, reason about, and communicate about fractions less than $\frac{1}{2}$?

For commentary on the above, see the Appendix: Authors' Video Reflections.

VIDEO CLIP 8f

Using Academic Language to Describe the Relationship Between the Numerator and Denominator in Fractions Less Than $\frac{1}{2}$

This clip begins with Makei describing the relationship between the numerator and denominator of fractions less than $\frac{1}{2}$. How does the teacher help him to articulate his idea? How does refining and charting Makei's observation provide opportunities for more students to understand this important idea?

For commentary on the above, see the Appendix: Authors' Video Reflections.

8. Repeat with all the fractions that they labeled that are greater than $\frac{1}{2}$ on the number lines.

VIDEO CLIP 8g

Reasoning About Fractions Greater Than $\frac{1}{2}$

After discussing the characteristics of fractions that are equal to and less than $\frac{1}{2}$, students identify fractions on their number lines that are greater than $\frac{1}{2}$. How does students' work with the fraction kits and number lines help them identify, reason about, and communicate about fractions greater than $\frac{1}{2}$?

For commentary on the above, see the Appendix: Authors' Video Reflections.

9. Last, give students some other fractions that are not in their Fraction Kits, such as $\frac{2}{5}$ and $\frac{10}{20}$, and ask them to decide where on the chart these fractions should go. Ask students to provide justification for each placement. For examples of student-completed number lines from this activity, see Figure 8–2.

VIDEO CLIP 8h

Reasoning About Fractions That Are Equal To, Less Than, and Greater Than $\frac{1}{2}$

After discussing the characteristics of fractions that are equal to, less than, and greater than $\frac{1}{2}$, Ms. Kretschmar asks students to consider fractions that are not on their number lines and decide whether they are equal to, less than, and greater than $\frac{1}{2}$. How does students' experience with Activity 8.1 provide them with strategies for comparing these fractions with $\frac{1}{2}$?

For commentary on the above, see the Appendix: Authors' Video Reflections.

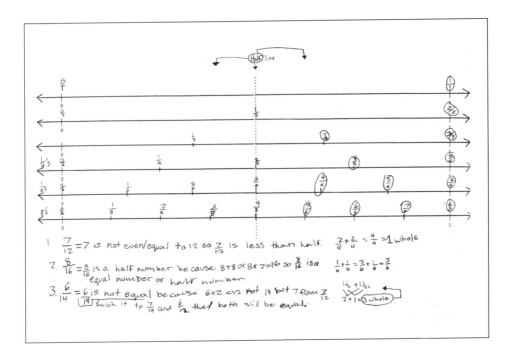

1. $\frac{7}{12}$ = 7 is not even/equal to 12 so $\frac{7}{12}$ is less than half. $\frac{2}{4} + \frac{2}{4} = \frac{4}{4} = 1$ whole

2. $\frac{8}{16} = \frac{8}{16}$ is a half number because 8+8 or 8×2=16 so $\frac{8}{16}$ is a $\frac{1}{6} + \frac{1}{6} = \frac{2}{6} + \frac{1}{6} = \frac{3}{6}$
   equal number or half number.

3. $\frac{6}{14} = 6$ is not equal because 6×2 =12 not 14 but 7 from $\frac{7}{12}$ $\frac{1\frac{1}{2} + 1\frac{1}{2} =}{2 + 1 = 3 \text{ whole}}$
   $\underline{14}$ swich it to $\frac{7}{14}$ and $\frac{6}{14}$ they both will be equal.

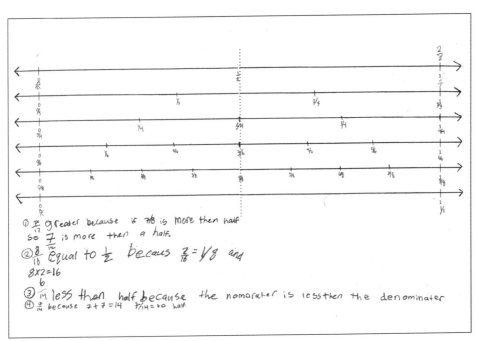

① $\frac{7}{12}$ greater because if 7/8 is more then half
   so $\frac{7}{12}$ is more then a half.

② $\frac{8}{16}$ equal to $\frac{1}{2}$ becaus $\frac{7}{16} = 1/8$ and
   8×2=16

③ $\frac{6}{14}$ less than half because the nomarater is lessthen the denominater

④ $\frac{7}{14}$ because 7+7 =14 7/14 = to half

Figure 8–2. Student-completed number lines.

8.2 Put in Order

Overview

In this activity from Burns (2007), students build on their experience with Activity 8.1: *More or Less Than $\frac{1}{2}$?* to place a set of fractions in order. By doing this as a whole-group activity, students hear their peers' reasoning explained in many different ways.

Materials

Fraction Cards (**Reproducibles 8c–8d**) or index cards with one fraction written on each card, 1 set per class

1. Start with the *Fraction Cards* labeled $\frac{1}{16}, \frac{1}{8}, \frac{3}{16}, \frac{1}{4}, \frac{3}{8}, \frac{1}{2}, \frac{5}{8}, \frac{3}{4}, \frac{15}{16}, \frac{1}{1}, \frac{9}{8}$, and $\frac{3}{2}$. (See Figure 8–3; also available as Reproducibles 8c–8d.)

2. Begin by placing the card with $\frac{1}{2}$ on it in the middle of the whiteboard ledger, or in a place that everyone can see, as a benchmark for students to work with.

3. Show the other cards one at a time, each time asking a student to place it where it belongs compared with $\frac{1}{2}$. As students place the cards, ask them to share their thinking about why they put cards where they did. Allow students to comment on the placements, explaining why they do or do not agree with the placements. As they become more familiar with the activity, use different sets of cards or present the cards in a different order.

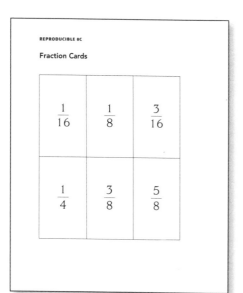

Figure 8–3. Fraction Cards (Reproducibles 8c and 8d)

8.3 Guess My Number

Overview

Materials
a means to display students' guesses to the whole class such as a whiteboard or overhead projector

This activity is from Olga Torres, an incredibly gifted teacher and mathematics educator. Although Olga taught *Guess My Number* using decimals, we found it to be a powerful activity when done with fractions. Not only does it help students reason about fraction values, but it also supports their understanding of fractions as numbers, and not just parts of pizzas.

1. Tell your students that you are thinking of a number between zero and one. Students may at first look surprised but, after the shock has passed, most likely someone will come up with $\frac{1}{2}$. If not, ask a question such as, "Are there any numbers between zero and one? What would you say if I gave each pair of you one piece of paper to share? How much would you each get?"

2. Start with a fairly familiar fraction such as $\frac{5}{8}$, but don't tell it to the students. Instead say, "My number is greater than one-half," and record like this: *n (my number)* $> \frac{1}{2}$.

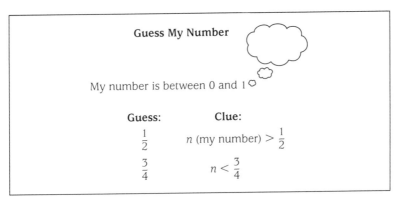

3. The students' next guess may be something like $\frac{3}{4}$; if so, say, "My number is less than three-fourths," and record like this: *n (my number)* $< \frac{3}{4}$. Continue with the guessing and recording until someone guesses your number.

4. You can easily differentiate this activity by limiting the denominators to those in the Fraction Kit or to common denominators such as halves, thirds, fourths, sixths, and eighths; using only unit fractions; using both fraction and decimal notation; and changing the range of possible numbers, perhaps telling students your number is between 1 and 2, instead of between 0 and 1.

Wrapping It Up

Providing opportunities for students to reason about fractional values lays an important foundation for further work involving fractions. The activities described in this chapter can help your students develop this necessary understanding and provide them with a framework for reasoning about any fractions they encounter. Comparing fractions with benchmarks such as 0, $\frac{1}{2}$, and 1 is a great place to start.

For More Information

For more information about helping students engage in discussions during mathematics class see, *Classroom Discussions in Math: A Teacher's Guide for Using Talk Moves to Support the Common Core and More*, Grades K–6, Third Edition by Suzanne H. Chapin, Catherine O'Connor, Nancy Canavan Anderson (2013).

Study Questions

After Reading Chapter 8

1. What information presented in the "Classroom Scenario," "What's the Math?," and "What's the Research?" sections was familiar to you or similar to your experience with students?

2. What information presented in the "Classroom Scenario," "What's the Math?," and "What's the Research?" sections was new or surprising to you?

3. Which of the Classroom Activities (Activity 8.1: *More or Less than* $\frac{1}{2}$?, Activity 8.2: *Put in Order*, and Activity 8.3: *Guess My Number*) do you plan to implement with your students?

After Trying One or More of the Activities

1. Describe the activity and any modifications you made to meet your students' needs and/or to align with your curriculum.

2. How did this activity add to your knowledge of what your students do and do not understand about strategies for comparing fractions?

3. What are your next steps for supporting your students' learning about comparing fractions?

Connections to *Beyond Invert & Multiply*

The foundational understandings introduced in *Beyond Pizzas & Pies, Second Edition*, are further developed in its companion resource, *Beyond Invert & Multiply*. We recommend pairing this chapter with Chapters 3, 4, 6, and 7 in *Beyond Invert & Multiply* to further your learning.

Acknowledgments

Our interest in the teaching and learning of fractions took hold when we were both doctoral students in the Graduate School of Education at the University of California, Berkeley. Under the direction of Geoffery Saxe and Maryl Gearhart, we participated in several research studies exploring students' understanding of, and difficulties with, fractions. Our work on these projects was instrumental to the development of our thinking about the teaching and learning of fractions. We would like to thank Geoff and Maryl for all of their thoughtful guidance over the years. In addition, we would like to thank our colleagues on these projects for the rich conversations about the teaching and learning of fractions, which furthered our thinking.

When we started work on the first edition of *Beyond Pizzas & Pies*, we didn't really have a clear vision of the final product. We knew we wanted to present common dilemmas/misconceptions that students have about fractions. We also knew we wanted to include a section about the mathematics involved, a review of relevant research, and a selection of activities that could be implemented in the classroom. Through the wonderful and patient guidance and suggestions provided by the folks at Math Solutions, in particular Doris Hirschhorn and Jamie Cross, the resource took shape. Doris and Jamie's comments were always clear, kind, and necessary. As we got further along in the process, Melissa Inglis-Elliott stepped in and was consistently supportive, answering our (many) questions in a timely manner and helping us to refine and fine-tune the text. Finally, Carolyn Felux was wonderfully supportive and encouraging throughout the writing and editing stages.

Eric Hsu, Associate Professor of Mathematics at San Francisco State University, provided a thoughtful review of the "What's the Math?" sections. Any errors that remain are our own.

With the publication of the second edition of *Beyond Pizzas & Pies*, our debt of gratitude to the wonderful people at Math Solutions has grown exponentially. Jamie Cross and Denise Botelho have been incredibly patient and thorough, especially as we finalized the text and video clips of the activities from the book. We so appreciated having Carolyn Felux, Patty Clark, Kelli Cook, and Patricio Dujan on site during the filming of the lessons on the DVD. (If you watch carefully, you may even catch a glimpse of them from time to time.)

We thank the crew at Friday's Films who treat the work of teaching and learning with tremendous respect and were a delight to work with.

Many teachers and students contributed to the research and activities in this book.

We thank administrators, Steve Sexton and Yanira Canizales, at Lighthouse Community Charter School in Oakland, California, for allowing us to bring a film crew into their school. The lessons included on the DVD would not have been possible without their support as well as the support and enthusiasm of the wonderful teachers at Lighthouse. Lauren Hofmayer, Laura Kretschmar, Emily Lee, Ben Seay, and Heather Thompson generously allowed us, and a film crew, to disrupt precious instructional time to prepare for and film the lessons on the DVD. We thank the parents and guardians for allowing their students to participate in the lessons. Most importantly, we thank the students for their hard work, persistence, and excitement about learning. Everyone who watches you will learn from your examples!

We owe a huge debt of gratitude to the many other teachers and students who have allowed us into their classrooms and have helped deepen our understanding of the teaching and learning of fractions. In addition, we'd like to thank the researchers whose work has contributed to our understanding of this challenging topic, as well as the chapters of this book. Last but not least, we thank our colleagues, families, and friends who have acted as sounding boards, proofreaders, and cheerleaders.

Reproducibles

Shading or Showing Fractional Parts: Unpartitioned

Date: _____

Name: _____

Shade $\frac{1}{2}$ of each shape.

Shade $\frac{1}{3}$ of each shape.

Show $\frac{1}{2}$ on the number line.

0   1

Show $\frac{1}{3}$ on the number line.

0   1

Shading or Showing Fractional Parts: Unpartitioned

Date: _____

Name: _____

Shade _____ of each shape.

Shade _____ of each shape.

Show _____ on the number line.

0   1

Show _____ on the number line.

0   1

Shading or Showing Fractional Parts: Partitioned

Date: _____

Name: _____

Shade $\frac{1}{10}$ of the rectangle.

Shade $\frac{1}{2}$ of the square.

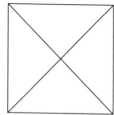

Shade $\frac{2}{3}$ of the hexagon.

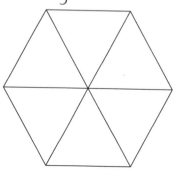

Shade $\frac{3}{8}$ of the circle.

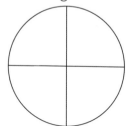

Show $\frac{1}{4}$ on the number line.

Show $\frac{1}{3}$ on the number line.

Shading or Showing Fractional Parts: Unequally Partitioned

Date: _____

Name: _____

Write a fraction to show how much of the large square is shaded. _____

Write a fraction to show how much of the large rectangle is shaded. _____

What fraction is shown by A? _____

What fraction is shown by B? _____

REPRODUCIBLE 1E

Part to Whole and Whole to Part

Date: _____

Name: _____

1. Start with the orange rod.

   a. Which rod is $\frac{1}{2}$ of the orange rod? _____
      How do you know?

   b. Which rod is $\frac{1}{5}$ of the orange rod? _____
      How do you know?

   c. Which rod is $\frac{1}{10}$ of the orange rod? _____
      How do you know?

2. Take out the brown rod.

   a. Which rod is $\frac{1}{2}$ of the brown rod? _____
      How do you know?

   b. Which rod is $\frac{1}{4}$ of the brown rod? _____
      How do you know?

   c. Which rod is $\frac{1}{8}$ of the brown rod? _____
      How do you know?

3. Take out the light-green rod.

    a. If the light-green rod is $\frac{1}{3}$, which rod is the whole?

    _____

       How do you know?

    b. If the light-green rod is $\frac{1}{3}$, which rod is $\frac{2}{3}$?

    _____

       How do you know?

4. Take out the white rod.

    a. If the white rod is $\frac{1}{5}$, which rod is the whole?

    _____

       How do you know?

    b. If the white rod is $\frac{1}{5}$, which rod is $\frac{2}{5}$? _____
       How do you know?

5. Take out the dark-green rod.

    a. If the dark-green rod is $\frac{3}{4}$, which rod is the whole?

    _____

       How do you know?

    b. If the dark-green rod is $\frac{2}{3}$, which rod is the whole?

    _____

       How do you know?

12-cm Number Lines

Date: _____

Name: _____

0 |——————————————————————————————————| 1

0 |——————————————————————————————————| 1

0 |——————————————————————————————————| 1

0 |——————————————————————————————————| 1

0 |——————————————————————————————————| 1

0 |——————————————————————————————————| 1

Measuring with Cuisenaire Rods

Date: _____

Name: _____

Item Being Measured	First Way	Second Way	Third Way
marker			
pencil			
book			

Centimeter-Squared Paper

Equivalent Fractions on the Number Line

Date: _____

Name: _____

Number	Equivalent Fractions on Your Number Line	Other Equivalent Fractions
0		
$\frac{1}{12}$		
$\frac{1}{6}$		
$\frac{1}{4}$		
$\frac{1}{3}$		
$\frac{5}{12}$		
$\frac{1}{2}$		
$\frac{7}{12}$		
$\frac{2}{3}$		
$\frac{3}{4}$		
$\frac{5}{6}$		

REPRODUCIBLE 3C (cont'd)

Number	Equivalent Fractions on Your Number Line	Other Equivalent Fractions
$\frac{11}{12}$		
1		
$1\frac{1}{12}$		
$1\frac{1}{6}$		
$1\frac{1}{4}$		
$1\frac{1}{3}$		
$1\frac{5}{12}$		
$1\frac{1}{2}$		
$1\frac{7}{12}$		
$1\frac{2}{3}$		
$1\frac{3}{4}$		
$1\frac{5}{6}$		
$1\frac{11}{12}$		
2		

Equivalent Fraction Cards

$1\dfrac{5}{7}$	$\dfrac{7}{3}$	$\dfrac{3}{10}$	$\dfrac{9}{30}$	$\dfrac{4}{5}$
$\dfrac{3}{4}$	$\dfrac{1}{25}$	$\dfrac{4}{100}$	$\dfrac{2}{3}$	$\dfrac{12}{7}$
$\dfrac{3}{21}$	$2\dfrac{1}{3}$	$\dfrac{50}{60}$	$\dfrac{8}{9}$	$\dfrac{32}{36}$

Equivalent Fraction Cards

$1\frac{2}{5}$	$\frac{6}{8}$	$\frac{16}{20}$
$\frac{8}{10}$	$\frac{7}{5}$	$\frac{1}{7}$
$1\frac{1}{4}$	$\frac{2}{4}$	$\frac{4}{5}$

$\frac{2}{16}$	$\frac{1}{8}$	
$\frac{6}{9}$	$\frac{5}{6}$	
$\frac{5}{4}$	$\frac{3}{6}$	

Brick by Brick

Date: _____

Name: _____

The brick company often has partial bricks left over from jobs and would like help figuring out how to use them. They know that two half-bricks will be the same size as one whole brick. In the space below, make a list of all the different ways to use the partial bricks so they don't go to waste.

1. Ways to make 1 whole brick:

$$\tfrac{1}{2} \textbf{ brick } + \tfrac{1}{2} \textbf{ brick}$$

2. Ways to make $\tfrac{1}{2}$ of a brick:

3. Ways to make $\tfrac{1}{4}$ of a brick:

4. Ways to make $\tfrac{1}{3}$ of a brick:

5. Ways to make $\frac{2}{3}$ of a brick:

6. Ways to make $\frac{3}{4}$ of a brick:

7. Ways to make $\frac{5}{8}$ of a brick:

8. Ways to make $1\frac{1}{2}$ bricks:

9. Ways to make 2 bricks:

Pattern Block Fractions

Date: _____

Name: _____

	Whole (hexagon)	Whole (rhombus)	Whole (trapezoid)	Whole (triangle)
hexagon				
trapezoid				
rhombus				
triangle				

REPRODUCIBLE 5A

"What Do You Call the _____?"

Date: _____

Name: _____

	What do you call the △	What do you call the ▱	What do you call the ⬓	What do you call the ⬡
when the ⬡ is the whole?				
when the ⬓ is the whole?				
when the ▱ is the whole?				
when the △ is the whole?				

Double Number Lines

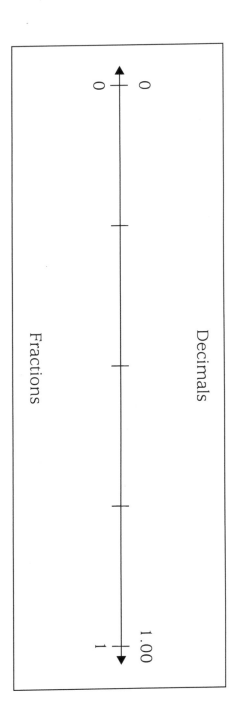

Fraction/Decimal Cards

$\dfrac{1}{10}$	0.1	$\dfrac{3}{10}$	0.3	$\dfrac{4}{5}$
0.8	$\dfrac{1}{25}$	0.04	$\dfrac{3}{4}$	0.75
$\dfrac{2}{5}$	0.4	$\dfrac{1}{5}$	0.2	$\dfrac{1}{2}$

Fraction/Decimal Cards

$\dfrac{7}{10}$	0.7	$\dfrac{3}{5}$
0.55	$\dfrac{1}{4}$	0.25
$\dfrac{7}{8}$	0.875	$\dfrac{1}{8}$
0.6	$\dfrac{9}{10}$	0.125
0.5	0.9	$\dfrac{11}{20}$

Fractions and Decimals on the Number Line

Date: _____

Name: _____

Directions: Use the number from your card to answer the following questions.

1. My number: _____
   An equivalent fraction or decimal: _____

2. Place your number and its equivalent on the number line below. How did you know where to place your numbers?

3. From the list below, choose at least 2 fractions and 2 decimals that are greater than your number and place them on the number line. How did you know where to place your numbers?

4. From the list below, choose at least 2 fractions and 2 decimals that are less than your number and place them on the number line. How did you know where to place your numbers?

$$\frac{1}{10}, \frac{1}{8}, \frac{7}{10}, \frac{1}{5}, \frac{1}{4}, \frac{3}{10}, \frac{2}{5}, \frac{11}{20}, \frac{1}{25}, \frac{3}{5}, \frac{3}{4}, \frac{1}{2}, \frac{7}{8}, \frac{4}{5}, \frac{9}{10}$$

0.25, 0.1, 0.7, 0.125, 0.9, 0.55, 0.75, 0.5, 0.8, 0.4, 0.875, 0.2, 0.6, 0.3, 0.04

Fractions and Decimals Flip Cards

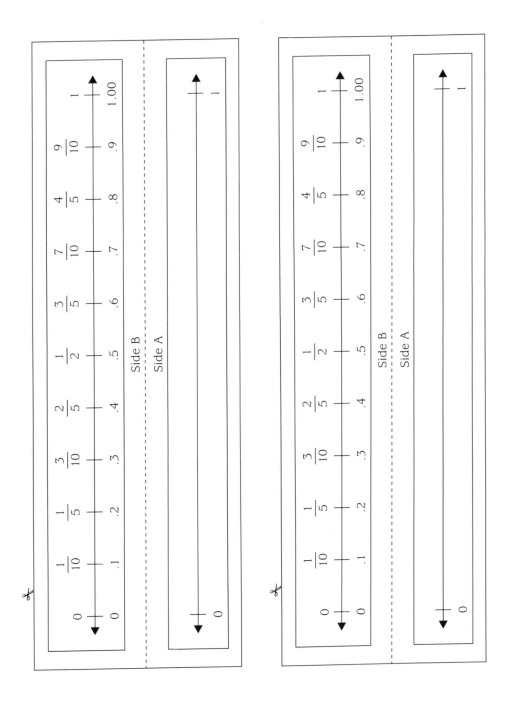

Fraction Representation Cards

Area model: circle

Number line

Measure

Area model: rectangle

Set model

Left Half of Number Line

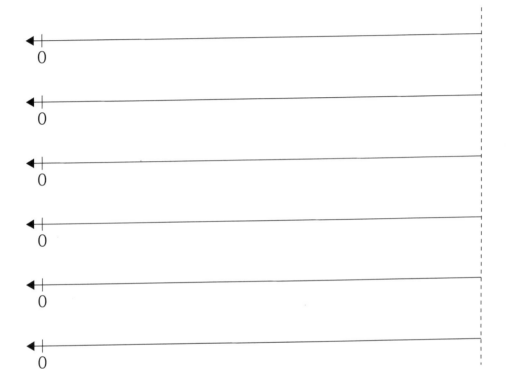

REPRODUCIBLE 8B

Right Half of Number Line

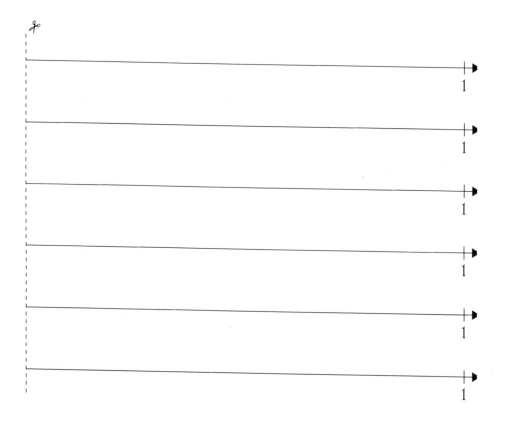

Fraction Cards

$\dfrac{1}{16}$	$\dfrac{1}{8}$	$\dfrac{3}{16}$
$\dfrac{1}{4}$	$\dfrac{3}{8}$	$\dfrac{5}{8}$

Fraction Cards

$\dfrac{1}{2}$	$\dfrac{3}{4}$	$\dfrac{15}{16}$
$\dfrac{1}{1}$	$\dfrac{9}{8}$	$\dfrac{3}{2}$

Left Half of Two-Unit Number Lines

Date: _____

Name: _____

0 ———————————————————————————————— 1

0 ———————————————————————————————— 1

0 ———————————————————————————————— 1

0 ———————————————————————————————— 1

0 ———————————————————————————————— 1

0 ———————————————————————————————— 1

Right Half of Two-Unit Number Lines

Date: _____

Name: _____

Authors' Video Reflections

Video Clip Number/ Title/Grade/Teacher	Page Number	Introduction	Observations
2a Introducing Activity 2.1: Number Line Activities with Cuisenaire Rods Grade 3/Mr. Seay	25	In this clip, which takes place at the beginning of Activity 2.1, we see the teacher, Mr. Seay, share something he observed in partner work: a "solution" for partitioning the unit interval on the number line in two parts. How does Mr. Seay's sharing of this observation help students' understanding?	An important aspect of partitioning any length, area, item, or group of objects into fractional parts is that the parts must be equal. Mr. Seay's demonstration of the incorrect solution acknowledges the part of the solution that was correct (the student had partitioned the unit interval into two parts) while reinforcing the necessity of having both parts be equal in length.
2b Splitting the Number Line in Half Grade 4/Ms. Lee	26	After partitioning the number line in half in Activity 2.1, two students in Ms. Lee's class share their thinking about how to partition the unit interval in half. What is the purpose of Ms. Lee's questioning?	Ms. Lee's questions serve to make Eduardo's and Astrid's thinking about why they chose the dark green rods to partition the number line in half public. Students often provide answers to questions during whole-group discussion but neglect to explain the rationale behind their answers. Ms. Lee's questions not only help Eduardo and Astrid become better at explaining their thinking to their classmates but also reinforce for the rest of the students the importance of partitioning the unit interval in its entirety.
2c The Purple Ones Work! Grade 4/Ms. Lee	27	In this clip, we see two students working on Step 3 of Activity 2.1: Find the rods that will partition the number line equally into $\frac{1}{3}$s. The students first try partitioning the unit interval into $\frac{1}{3}$s with the yellow rods because when they previously worked with a fraction kit, the yellow ones were the $\frac{1}{3}$s. How does the students' thinking change as they work to solve the problem? Why do the students decide that the purple rods, not the yellow rods, work? How do they come to this conclusion?	As the students use the materials to find the rods that partition the unit interval into three equal parts, they find that their first attempt (using the yellow rods) doesn't work, because three yellow rods is much longer than the unit interval. As they try different rods, they find that the purple rods work, because they are the rods that when iterated three times, are the same length as the unit interval. Even after determining that the purple rods work, the boys go on to eliminate the other rods, explaining that some are too short while others are too long. The students use the materials to create a clear, visual model of the definition of $\frac{1}{3}$ by showing how it is the quantity formed by 1 part when a whole is partitioned into b (in this case 3) equal parts.

Video Clip Number/ Title/Grade/Teacher	Page Number	Introduction	Observations
2d Lizette's Strategy for Finding the Rod That Is $\frac{1}{3}$ of the Unit Interval Grade 4/Ms. Lee	27	In this clip from Activity 2.1, Ms. Lee asks Lizette to share how she partitioned the unit interval into $\frac{1}{3}$s. How does Lizette justify her use of the pink (purple) rods? What important idea, tied to the definition of a unit fraction, does Lizette draw on in her explanation?	As with the students shown in Video Clip 2c, Lizette's explanation for why she used the pink (purple) rods to partition the unit interval into $\frac{1}{3}$s provides a clear, visual model of the definition of $\frac{1}{3}$ by showing how it is the quantity formed by 1 part when a whole is partitioned into b (in this case 3) equal parts.
2e Labeling the Number Line Grade 3/Mr. Seay	28	In this clip from Activity 2.1, we see Mr. Seay demonstrating for students how to label the number line after the unit interval has been partitioned into $\frac{1}{3}$s. How does Mr. Seay's explicit use of the chart and the large number line help students' understanding?	Mr. Seay's use of the chart and number line serve two important purposes for his third-grade students. First, the chart helps students see the relationship between the number of rods needed to partition the unit interval (in this case, 3) and the name of one of the rods ($\frac{1}{3}$). The second purpose addresses how to label the fractions on the number line. When students first transition from using materials like fraction kits to representing fractions on the number line, they may need explicit instruction on *how* and *where* to write the fractions. While it is true that in this context any one of the purple rods could be labeled $\frac{1}{3}$ (and that label could be written anywhere on the rod) this is not the case when labeling the fractions on the number line. The number line is a distance model, meaning that as the rods are iterated on the number line, the label for $\frac{1}{3}$ goes at the end of the first rod, the label $\frac{2}{3}$ goes at the end of the second rod, and the label $\frac{3}{3}$ goes at the end of the third rod.

(continued)

Video Clip Number/ Title/Grade/Teacher	Page Number	Introduction	Observations
2f Using Knowledge of $\frac{1}{2}$ to Find $\frac{1}{6}$s Grade 4/Ms. Lee	29	In this clip, we see Marcela and Camilo describing how they found the rods that are $\frac{1}{6}$ of the unit interval. What important fraction concept does Marcela's reasoning support?	Marcela's strategy of using the rod that equals $\frac{1}{2}$ to find the rods that equal $\frac{1}{6}$ highlights her understanding of the multiplicative relationship between $\frac{1}{2}$s, $\frac{1}{3}$s, and $\frac{1}{6}$s. She finds that three red rods are the same length as the rod that is $\frac{1}{2}$ of the unit interval. Since she knows that "three plus three equals six" and "a half plus a half is one whole," she is able to determine that the rods that are $\frac{1}{3}$ of the half are $\frac{1}{6}$ of the whole.
2g What Do You Know About Numbers Between 0 and 1? Grade 3/Mr. Seay	30	Before launching Activity 2.2, Mr. Seay asks his third graders to share what they think about the numbers between 0 and 1. What do students seem to know about these numbers?	By starting with this question, Mr. Seay finds out that his students are not aware that there are numbers between 0 and 1. They also indicate a lack of understanding about the number line, as many students suggest placing 0 between 0 and 1, and another student suggests that the number 1 should be written at the same place.
2h What Are We Learning About Numbers Between 0 and 1? Grade 3/Mr. Seay	31	During Activity 2.2, Mr. Seay asks students if they are beginning to find numbers between 0 and 1. How do students respond? How does this activity support students' understanding of fractions?	During the middle of Activity 2.2, Mr. Seay revisits the question from the beginning of the lesson, "What are the numbers between 0 and 1?" His students indicate that they are beginning to think about the numbers between 0 and 1, although we can hear several students suggest that they are not numbers, but instead they are fractions. Hearing this, Mr. Seay explicitly states that they are indeed fractions, and that fractions are actually numbers on the number line.

Video Clip Number/ Title/Grade/Teacher	Page Number	Introduction	Observations
2i Revisiting the Question, "What Are the Numbers Between 0 and 1?" Grade 3/Mr. Seay	32	After students have completed Activity 2.2, Mr. Seay revisits the question from the beginning of the lesson, "What are the numbers between 0 and 1?" How do students' answers differ from the ones they gave at the beginning of the lesson (see Video Clip 2g)? What experiences are students drawing from to name several fractions that are between 0 and 1?	In stark contrast to the beginning of the lesson when students indicated very little understanding of numbers between 0 and 1, after partitioning their number lines during Activity 2.2, students suggest several numbers that are between 0 and 1, such as $\frac{1}{2}$, $\frac{1}{3}$, $\frac{2}{3}$, $\frac{1}{4}$, $\frac{2}{4}$, and $\frac{3}{4}$. Students' answers stem directly from Activity 2.1, as they reference fractions that were encountered when partitioning their number lines with the Cuisenaire rods.
3a Introducing Activity 3.1: Measuring with Cuisenaire Rods Grade 4/Ms. Thompson	50	In this clip, Ms. Thompson introduces her fourth graders to Activity 3.1. Students make an estimate of the length of a marker using brown rods as their measurement unit. What does Ms. Thompson learn about her students' understanding of fractions and measurement during this introduction?	Of the students who volunteer an estimate for the length of the marker, only Diego suggests using a fraction to name the length in terms of brown rods. Several students say that they know the marker is more than one, but less than two, brown rods long. Their answers indicate an intuitive understanding of a measurement between 1 and 2, but at this point in the lesson, they are unsure what to call it.

(continued)

APPENDIX • AUTHORS' VIDEO REFLECTIONS 181

Video Clip Number/ Title/Grade/Teacher	Page Number	Introduction	Observations
3b "How Many Brown Rods Long Is the Marker?" Grade 4/Ms. Thompson	51	Just before this clip, Edwin states that the marker was one brown and one purple rod long. Ms. Thompson agrees with Edwin and then calls Sarah up to name the purple rod in relation to the brown rod. Sarah provides the correct fraction name for the purple rod but is not able to provide a complete answer to the question, "How many brown rods long is the marker?" How does Ms. Thompson press her students to come to a complete answer to the question?	During this clip Ms. Thompson's students struggle to consolidate the lengths of the different rods that were used to measure the marker. Instead of stopping after Sarah correctly names the purple rod in relation to the brown rod, Ms. Thompson asks another student to explain why Sarah names the purple rod as one-half of the brown rod. She then questions the class ("Is this marker one-half of a brown rod?") to reinforce the idea that while the purple rod is indeed one-half of the brown rod, the length of the entire marker is one whole brown rod plus another one-half of a brown rod. She then demonstrates for students how to write the correct measurement of $1\frac{1}{2}$ brown rods.
3c Different Names for the Remainder Length Grade 4/Ms. Thompson	51	This clip opens with Ms. Thompson reminding students of their task for Activity 3.1. Then we see a group of fourth graders working on the task—specifically how to measure the "remainder length" of the marker. How can their explorations with the different rods be used to support their understanding of equivalent fractions?	As students explore the different rods that can be used to measure the remainder length, they are discovering important relationships among the rods. They find that the purple rod is also the same length as four white rods, two red rods, and one white rod plus one light green rod. While the students in this clip haven't yet found the fraction names for the different rods, their discoveries of the relationships among the different rods support the understanding that equivalent fractions are different ways to name the same length. View Video Clip 3f to see Diego share his "discoveries" about equivalent fractions with his classmates.

Video Clip Number/ Title/Grade/Teacher	Page Number	Introduction	Observations
3d What Do We Call Four White Rods? Grade 4/Ms. Thompson	54	Emily and her partner have found that the marker is one brown rod and four white rods long, but she is unsure of what to name the white rods. How does Ms. Thompson guide the students to help them name the white rods? How can Ms. Thompson's approach help students create a generalization about naming fractions?	Ms. Thompson begins by asking Emily how many white rods are the same length as one brown rod. After Emily answers, "eight," Ms. Thompson suggests Emily use the chart to help her determine the fractional name for the white rods. Even though eighths are not represented on the chart, Emily is able to use the information about naming fractions ("If the part is $\frac{1}{n}$ you need n to make the whole") to determine that each white rod is one-eighth of the brown rod, thus the marker is $1\frac{4}{8}$ brown rods long.
3e Making Monica's Thinking Public Grade 4/Ms. Thompson	54	Ms. Thompson calls on Monica to show the class how she determined that the brown rod and four white rods was $1\frac{4}{8}$. How does Ms. Thompson make Monica's thinking public and accessible to the rest of the class?	After Monica provides the correct answer of $1\frac{4}{8}$, Ms. Thompson calls her up to explain how she arrived at her answer. Ms. Thompson knows that some students may not fully understand why $1\frac{4}{8}$ is the correct answer so she presses Monica to justify her response using the rods. By counting the $\frac{1}{8}$s ("One-eighth, two-eighths, three-eighths, four-eighths"), Ms. Thompson also helps the class understand how $\frac{4}{8}$ is made up of four $\frac{1}{8}$s.
3f Using the Rods to Show How $\frac{1}{2}$, $\frac{2}{4}$, and $\frac{4}{8}$ Are Equivalent Grade 4/Ms. Thompson	55	In this clip, we see Diego share something he noticed about the equivalency between one purple rod, two red rods, and four white rods, all of which equal $\frac{1}{2}$ of the brown rod. Ms. Thompson follows Diego's discovery by calling on Celeste to explain Diego's thinking. How do the materials support Diego and Celeste as they share their thinking with their classmates?	The explorations with the rods led Diego to notice that the different ways of measuring the remainder length used different rods, but all are equivalent to $\frac{1}{2}$. Even though using the different rods resulted in different fraction names for the remainder length, ($\frac{1}{2}$, $\frac{2}{4}$, and $\frac{4}{8}$), it did not change the length being measured. Understanding that equivalent fractions are merely different names for the same value is an incredibly important concept for students to understand, but is often challenging for them to grasp. See the "What's the Research?" section in Chapter 3 (p. 47) for more on this topic.

(continued)

Video Clip Number/ Title/Grade/Teacher	Page Number	Introduction	Observations
5a Reviewing the Names of the Pattern Blocks Grade 3/Ms. McNamara	86	In this clip, we see students reviewing the names of the pattern blocks used in Activity 5.1. What teacher moves are used in this clip to ensure that all students are able to contribute to the review?	To provide time for all students to consider the answer to her question regarding the names of the shapes, Ms. McNamara tells students she is asking a "thinking question." This move can be especially beneficial for students who need to translate the name of the shape from their native language into English. After allowing several seconds of thinking time, Ms. McNamara then instructs students to "turn and talk" and share their answer with a partner. This move provides an opportunity for students to hear the name of the shape if they don't know it already and practice saying the name of the shape to a classmate. Finally the choral, or group response, provides an opportunity for all students to say and hear the shape's name one more time, with the additional support of their classmates.
5b Introducing Activity 5.1: Pattern Block Fractions, Version 2 Grade 3/Ms. McNamara	87	In this clip, we see the introduction to Activity 5.1. Students are shown a triangle and asked to give it a fraction name. After several ideas have been presented, Ms. McNamara reminds students that to determine the fraction name of the triangle, they need to know which shape is the whole. How does this introduction prepare students for the activity?	Beginning Activity 5.1 with this question provides students with a dilemma to be solved. As students work on the activity, they learn that a fraction name such as *one-sixth* is not just a label given to a block but defines a relationship between the block designated as the part and the block designated as the whole. The question, "What fraction is the triangle?" can only be answered in terms of what the triangle is a fraction of.

Video Clip Number/ Title/Grade/Teacher	Page Number	Introduction	Observations
5c What Do You Call the Triangle When the Trapezoid Is the Whole? Grade 3/Ms. McNamara	88	After naming the triangle when the hexagon is the whole, students are asked to name the triangle when the trapezoid is the whole. We see Jorge using the giant pattern blocks to justify his answer of $\frac{1}{3}$. How do the materials support the third graders' understanding of this definition of a fraction from the Common Core: "Understand a fraction $\frac{1}{b}$ as the quantity formed by 1 part when a whole is partitioned into b equal parts?"	As Jorge uses the materials to justify his answer that the triangle is $\frac{1}{3}$ of the trapezoid, he is able to show how three triangles fit on the trapezoid, concluding that one triangle is $\frac{1}{3}$ of the trapezoid. The pattern blocks provide a geometric example of the Common Core definition of a fraction because the whole (in this case, the trapezoid) is partitioned into b (3) equal parts and one of those equal parts is $\frac{1}{b}$ $\left(\frac{1}{3}\right)$.
5d Stephanie's Use of the Pattern Blocks to Support Her Reasoning Grade 3/Ms. McNamara	89	This clip takes place after students have worked at their table to complete their own charts. We see Stephanie using the giant pattern blocks to justify her answer of $\frac{1}{3}$. How do the materials support the third graders' understanding of this definition of a fraction from the Common Core: "Understand a fraction $\frac{1}{b}$ as the quantity formed by 1 part when a whole is partitioned into b equal parts?"	When Stephanie uses the giant pattern blocks to justify her answer of $\frac{1}{3}$, she provides another example of the Common Core definition of a fraction: "Understand a fraction $\frac{1}{b}$ as the quantity formed by 1 part when a whole is partitioned into b equal parts." In this situation, the whole is now the hexagon, yet when it is partitioned into b equal parts one of those equal parts is $\frac{1}{b}$ $\left(\frac{1}{3}\right)$.

(continued)

Video Clip Number/ Title/Grade/Teacher	Page Number	Introduction	Observations
5e What Do You Call the Rhombus When the Trapezoid Is the Whole? Grade 3/Ms. McNamara	90	In this clip, we first see Mahalya and Haran trying to figure out what to call the rhombus when the trapezoid is the whole. Then we see this being discussed as a whole class. In the whole-class discussion, $\frac{1}{2}$ and 2 are suggested, neither of which is the correct answer. How does Ms. McNamara honor students' thinking while encouraging them to build on their understanding of unit fractions to move toward the correct answer the girls came to, $\frac{2}{3}$?	In response to Warren's suggestion that the rhombus is $\frac{1}{2}$ of the trapezoid, Ms. McNamara reminds students that if a given block is $\frac{1}{2}$ of another block, then the block that is the whole is twice the size as the block that is $\frac{1}{2}$. She then acknowledges what Warren was likely noticing that two triangles fit on top of the rhombus, leaving room for one more triangle to complete the trapezoid. Matthew and Lizzeth then help the class come to the understanding that the rhombus, which is the same size as two triangles (or two $\frac{1}{3}$s), is $\frac{2}{3}$ of the trapezoid.
5f Is $\frac{1}{2}$ Always Greater Than $\frac{1}{3}$? Grade 3/Ms. McNamara	91	This clip takes place after students have completed Activity 5.1. Pattern Block Fractions, Version 2. Ms. McNamara asks students to respond to the statement, "$\frac{1}{2}$ is always greater than $\frac{1}{3}$." How does Matthew draw on his experience with Activity 5.1 to explain that the size of the whole matters and that, in some cases, $\frac{1}{3}$ may be bigger than $\frac{1}{2}$?	While completing the chart in Activity 5.1, students found that the blocks had different fraction names depending on the size of the block being used as the whole. For example, the triangle was $\frac{1}{2}$ of the rhombus, $\frac{1}{3}$ of the trapezoid, and $\frac{1}{6}$ of the hexagon. Students also found that when the hexagon was the whole the trapezoid was the half, and when the rhombus was the whole the triangle was the half. Matthew explains that the statement, "One-half is always bigger than one-third" is true when comparing $\frac{1}{2}$ and $\frac{1}{3}$ "on the same whole" but if $\frac{1}{2}$ and $\frac{1}{3}$ are on different wholes, then $\frac{1}{3}$ can be bigger.

Video Clip Number/ Title/Grade/Teacher	Page Number	Introduction	Observations
8a Introducing Activity 8.1: More or Less Than $\frac{1}{2}$? Grade 5/Ms. Kretschmar	134	In this clip, we see Ms. Kretschmar introducing her students to Activity 8.1. She makes a point of asking students to make sure she "did her homework," and made number lines with a unit distance that is the same length as the "whole" piece from the fraction kits they made during a previous lesson. Why is it important that students make this comparison?	Before her students use the pieces from their fraction kits to partition their number lines, it is essential that they understand that the halves (thirds, fourths, sixths, etc.) from the fraction kit can only be used to represent halves (thirds, fourths, sixths, etc.) of a unit interval that is the same length as the whole from their fraction kits. This step at the beginning of Activity 8.1 should not be skipped or rushed. It is necessary to further reinforce the important idea that the labels on the fraction kit pieces ($\frac{1}{2}$, $\frac{1}{3}$, $\frac{1}{4}$, etc.) represent a relationship between each piece and the strip designated as the whole, as well as the length of the unit interval on the number line.
8b Labeling the Number Line Grade 5/Ms. Kretschmar	135	In this clip, we see Ms. Kretschmar modeling for students how to partition and label the number line using the $\frac{1}{2}$ pieces from their fraction kits. Ms. Kretschmar is very explicit about where to place the numbers $\frac{1}{2}$ and $\frac{2}{2}$ on the number line. Why might labeling the number line be challenging for students as they transition from working with the fraction kit to the number line?	When students label pieces from a fraction kit, where they write each fraction does not matter. Students typically label their pieces in the middle of the strip, as shown here: However, as students use their fraction kit pieces to label their number lines, it is essential that they make the tick mark for each fraction at the end of the corresponding strip, because the value of each number on the number line is determined by its distance from 0. Instead of labeling $\frac{1}{2}$ anywhere between 0 and the tick mark for $\frac{1}{2}$, on the number line $\frac{1}{2}$ can only be written at one location, that is, the distance at which the unit interval (the distance from 0 to 1) is partitioned into two equivalent lengths, as shown here:

(continued)

Video Clip Number/ Title/Grade/Teacher	Page Number	Introduction	Observations
8c Fractions That Equal $\frac{1}{2}$ Grade 5/Ms. Kretschmar	137	In this clip, students have already used their fraction kits to partition their number lines. We now see several students share their ideas about fractions that are equal to $\frac{1}{2}$. How does students' work with the fraction kits and number lines help them identify, reason about, and communicate about fractions equal to $\frac{1}{2}$?	By using their fraction kit pieces to partition the number lines, students are able to see how several fractions ($\frac{1}{2}$, $\frac{2}{4}$, $\frac{3}{6}$, $\frac{4}{8}$) are all the same distance from 0 and thus, equivalent. Writing the fractions that students named on the chart allows students to focus on the relationship between the numerator and denominator of these fractions. This attention to the relationship between numerators and denominators of the fractions on the chart that equal $\frac{1}{2}$ provides students with a foundation from which to reason about all fractions equal to $\frac{1}{2}$.
8d Describing the Relationship Between the Numerator and Denominator in Fractions Equal To $\frac{1}{2}$ Grade 5/Ms. Kretschmar and Ms. McNamara	137	In this clip, Ms. Kretschmar revisits an observation made by Leo and RaSean that, in fractions equal to one-half, the "numinator [sic] is gonna be half of that number [the denominator]." Ms. Kretschmar calls on several students to repeat this idea and charts students' responses. How does the teacher's move of asking students to repeat Leo and RaSean's observation create opportunities for more students to understand this important idea?	The relationship between the numerators and denominators in fractions that equal $\frac{1}{2}$ can be expressed in multiple ways. After Leo suggests that the "numinator [sic] is gonna be half of that number [the denominator]," we hear Natalie, Laura, and ReSean restate Leo's idea. In this way, students are provided multiple opportunities to hear this observation presented. Natalie then presents another way to think about this relationship: If you multiply the numerator by two, you get the denominator. While these two ideas are mathematically equivalent, they may not appear so to students. Taking students' observations a bit farther, one could represent them algebraically. Leo and ReSean's observation could be represented as $n = \frac{1}{2}d$, while Natalie's observation could be represented as $2n = d$.

Video Clip Number/ Title/Grade/Teacher	Page Number	Introduction	Observations
8e Reasoning About Fractions Less Than $\frac{1}{2}$ Grade 5/Ms. Kretschmar	138	After discussing the characteristics of fractions that equal $\frac{1}{2}$, students identify fractions on their number lines that are less than $\frac{1}{2}$. How does students' work with the fraction kits and number lines help them identify, reason about, and communicate about fractions less than $\frac{1}{2}$?	By using their fraction kit pieces to partition the number lines, students were able to see how several fractions ($\frac{0}{2}$, $\frac{1}{3}$, $\frac{2}{8}$) were all between 0 and $\frac{1}{2}$ and thus, less than $\frac{1}{2}$. Writing the fractions that students named on the chart allows students to focus on the relationship between the numerator and denominator of these fractions. This attention to the relationship between numerators and denominators of the fractions on the chart that are less than $\frac{1}{2}$ provides students with a foundation from which to reason about all fractions less than $\frac{1}{2}$.
8f Using Academic Language to Describe the Relationship Between the Numerator and Denominator in Fractions Less Than $\frac{1}{2}$ Grade 5/Ms. Kretschmar	138	This clip begins with Makei describing the relationship between the numerator and denominator of fractions less than $\frac{1}{2}$. How does the teacher help him to articulate his idea? How does refining and charting Makei's observation provide opportunities for more students to understand this important idea?	Explaining one's thinking can be challenging for students, especially when they are talking about a complex topic like fractions. As Makei begins his explanation by stating, "If the *number* is half . . . ," Ms. Kretschmar, knowing that the number Makei is referring to is the numerator (and also knowing that many students may not understand that Makei is referring the numerator), prompts him to refine his statement using academic language. Continuing with his observation, Makei refers to the denominator as "the whole number." Again, Ms. Kretschmar provides him with the correct term (*denominator*) to make sure his observation is accurate and accessible to his classmates.

Video Clip Number/ Title/Grade/Teacher	Page Number	Introduction	Observations
8g Reasoning About Fractions Greater Than $\frac{1}{2}$ Grade 5/Ms. Kretschmar	139	After discussing the characteristics of fractions that are equal to and less than $\frac{1}{2}$, students identify fractions on their number lines that are greater than $\frac{1}{2}$. How does students' work with the fraction kits and number lines help them identify, reason about, and communicate about fractions greater than $\frac{1}{2}$?	By using their fraction kit pieces to partition the number lines, students are able to see how several fractions ($\frac{7}{8}$, $\frac{2}{6}$, $\frac{4}{6}$, $\frac{6}{8}$) are all farther from 0 than $\frac{1}{2}$ and thus, greater than $\frac{1}{2}$. Writing the fractions that students named on the chart allows students to focus on the relationship between the numerator and denominator of these fractions. This attention to the relationship between numerators and denominators of the fractions on the chart that are greater than $\frac{1}{2}$ provides students with a foundation from which to reason about all fractions greater than $\frac{1}{2}$.
8h Reasoning About Fractions That Are Equal To, Less Than, and Greater Than $\frac{1}{2}$ Grade 5/Ms. Kretschmar	140	After discussing the characteristics of fractions that are equal to, less than, and greater than $\frac{1}{2}$, Ms. Kretschmar asks students to consider fractions that are not on their number lines and decide whether they are equal to, less than, and greater than $\frac{1}{2}$. How does students' experience with Activity 8.1 provide them with strategies for comparing these fractions with $\frac{1}{2}$?	Working with the fraction kits and number lines allows students to generalize what they learned about the characteristics of fractions that are equal to, less than, and greater than $\frac{1}{2}$. Even though students only worked with a small sampling of fractions in Activity 8.1, we see how they are able to apply their observations to additional fractions that they did not encounter during this activity. Reasoning about fractions in comparison to a benchmark such as $\frac{1}{2}$ is an excellent way to develop and apply fraction sense.

References

Armstrong, Barbara E., and Carol N. Larson. 1995. Students' Use of Part–Whole and Direct Comparison Strategies for Comparing Partitioned Rectangles. *Journal for Research in Mathematics Education* 26: 2–19.

Ball, Deborah Loewenberg. 1992. Magical Hopes: Manipulatives and the Reform of Math Education. *American Educator* 16(2): 14–18, 46–48.

———. 1993. Halves, Pieces, and Twoths: Constructing Representational Contexts in Teaching Fractions. In *Rational Numbers: An Integration of Research*, eds. Thomas P. Carpenter, Elizabeth Fennema, and Thomas A. Romberg, 157–96. Hillsdale, NJ: Erlbaum.

Bobis, Janette. 2007. The Empty Number Line: A Useful Tool or Just Another Procedure? *Teaching Children Mathematics* 13(8): 410–23.

Bright, George M., Merlyn Behr, Thomas R. Post, and Ipke Wachsmuth. 1988. Identifying fractions on number lines. *Journal for Research in Mathematics Education,* 19(3): 215–32.

Burns, Marilyn. 2007. *About Teaching Mathematics: A K–8 Resource.* 3d ed. Sausalito, CA: Math Solutions.

Chapin, Suzanne H., Catherine O'Conner, and Nancy Anderson. 2013. *Classroom Discussions in Math: A Teacher's Guide for Using Talk Moves to Support the Common Core and More, Grades K–6: A Multimedia Professional Learning Resource.* 2d ed. Sausalito, CA: Math Solutions.

Chapin, Suzanne H., and Art Johnson. 2006. *Math Matters: Understanding the Math You Teach, Grades K–8.* 2d ed. Sausalito, CA: Math Solutions.

Cramer, Kathleen. 2003. Using a Translation Model for Curriculum Development and Classroom Instruction. In *Beyond Constructivism. Models and Modeling Perspectives on Mathematics Problem Solving, Learning, and Teaching*, eds. Richard Lesh and Helen M. Doerr, 449–63. Mahwah, NJ: Erlbaum.

Cramer, Kathleen A., Thomas R. Post, and Robert C. delMas. 2002. Initial Fraction Learning by Fourth- and Fifth-Grade Students: A Comparison of the Effects of Using Commercial Curricula with the Effects of Using the Rational Number Project Curriculum. *Journal for Research in Mathematics Education* 33(2): 111–44.

Davydov, V.V., and Z.H. Tsetkovich. 1991. On the Objective Origin of the Concept of Fractions. *Focus on Learning Problems in Mathematics* 13: 13–61.

Driscoll, Mark J. 1999. *Fostering Algebraic Thinking: A Guide for Teachers, Grades 6–10.* Portsmouth, NH: Heinemann.

Falkner, Karen P., Linda Levi, and Thomas P. Carpenter. 1999. Children's Understanding of Equality: A Foundation for Algebra. *Teaching Children Mathematics* 6(4): 232–36.

Fosnot, Catherine T., and Maarten Dolk. 2002. *Young Mathematicians at Work: Constructing Fractions, Decimals, and Percents.* Portsmouth, NH: Heinemann.

Gomez, Emiliano. 2009. Why Are Fractions So Useful at Predicting Success in Math? Talk presented at the California Mathematics Council Annual Conference, Monterey, CA, December, 2009.

Hiebert, James. 1984. Children's Mathematics Learning: The Struggle to Link Form and Understanding. *Elementary School Journal* 84: 497–513.

Kloosterman, Peter. 2010. Mathematics Skills of 17-Year-Olds in the United States: 1978 to 2004. *Journal for Research in Mathematics Education* 41(1): 20–51.

Lamon, Susan. J. 2007. Rational Numbers and Proportional Reasoning: Toward a Theoretical Framework for Research. In *Second Handbook of Research on Mathematics Teaching and Learning*, ed. Frank Lester, 629–67. Reston, VA: NCTM.

———. 2005. *Teaching Fractions and Ratios for Understanding: Essential Content Knowledge and Instructional Strategies for Teachers.* 2d. ed. Hillsdale, NJ: Lawrence Erlbaum.

Lesh, Richard, Thomas R. Post, and Merlyn J. Behr. 1987. Representations and Translations Among Representations in Mathematics Learning and Problem Solving. In *Problems of Representations in the Teaching and Learning of Mathematics*, ed. C. Janvier, 33–40. Hillsdale, NJ: Lawrence Erlbaum.

Mack, Nancy. 2001. Building on Informal Knowledge Through Instruction in a Complex Content Domain: Partitioning, Units, and Understanding Multiplication of Fractions. *Journal for Research in Mathematics Education* 32(3): 267–95.

———. 1995. Confounding Whole Number and Fraction Concepts When Building on Informal Knowledge. *Journal for Research in Mathematics Education* 26: 422–41.

———. 1990. Learning Fractions with Understanding: Building on Informal Knowledge. *Journal for Research in Mathematics Education* 21: 16–32.

MacGregor, Mollie, and Kaye Stacey. 1999. A Flying Start to Algebra. *Teaching Children Mathematics* 6(2): 78–85.

Math Pathways and Pitfalls, www.wested.org/cs/we/view/pj/81.

McNamara, Julie Clare. 2006. Using a Measurement Model to Support Students' Development of Fraction Understanding. Unpublished doctoral dissertation, University of California, Berkeley.

National Council of Teachers of Mathematics. 2006. *Curriculum Focal Points for Prekindergarten Through Grade 8 Mathematics.* Reston, VA: NCTM.

———. 2000. *Principles and Standards for School Mathematics.* Reston, VA: NCTM.

National Research Council. 2001. *Adding It Up: Helping Children Learn Mathematics,* eds. Jeremy Kilpatrick, Jane Swafford, and Bradford Findell. Washington, DC: National Academy Press.

Reys, Barbara J., Ok-Kyeong Kim, and Jennifer M. Bay. 1999. Establishing Fraction Benchmarks. *Mathematics Teaching in the Middle School* 4(8): 530–32.

Saxe, Geoffrey B., Edward V. Taylor, Clifton McIntosh, and Maryl Gearhart. 2005. Representing Fractions with Standard Notation: A Developmental Analysis. *Journal for Research in Mathematics Education* 36(2): 137–57.

Saxe, Geoffrey B., Meghan M. Shaughnessy, Ann Shannon, Jennifer M. Langer-Osuna, Ryan Chinn, and Maryl Gearhart. 2007. Learning About Fractions as Points on a Number Line. In *The Learning of Mathematics: Sixty-Ninth Yearbook,* eds. W. Gary Martin, Marilyn E. Strutchens, and Portia C. Elliott, 221–37. Reston, VA: NCTM.

Shaughnessy, Meghan M. 2009. Students' Flexible Use of Multiple Representations for Rational Number: Decimals, Fractions, Parts of Area, and Number Line. Unpublished doctoral dissertation, University of California, Berkeley.

U.S. Department of Education. 2008. *Foundations for Success: The Final Report of the National Mathematics Advisory Panel.*

Van de Walle, John, Karen S. Karp, and Jennifer Bay-Williams. 2009. *Elementary and Middle School Mathematics: Teaching Developmentally.* 7th ed. Columbus, OH: Allyn & Bacon.

Index